I0521639

BOUND ~~HOMELESS~~

CHOOSING A MINDSET FOR LIFELONG GROWTH

GRIFFIN FURLONG

Boundless
Copyright 2022 Griffin Furlong
All rights reserved

Published in the United States of America

Book layout: Abraham Obafemi Emmanuel
Editor: Kathleen Tracy

ebook ISBN: 979-8-9864138-2-2
Paperback ISBN: 979-8-9864138-0-8
Hardback ISBN: 979-8-9864138-1-5

To Mom:
    You read to me in the hospital bed, and now I write to you in heaven.

ACKNOWLEDGEMENTS

A special thank you to my good friend, Yianni Hantzopoulos. You were there with me during the initial concept of the book and you believed in me every step of the way. Thank you for all the edits, hours, phone calls, and helping me navigate through my battle with perfectionism.

I would also like to thank my friend, and coworker buddy, Abby Brayton, for making my book cover come to life and being there for me whenever I needed a helping hand. Your sacrifice and patience during your own busy schedule was honorable.

Thank you to my entire family, thank you Sean and dad for being my teammates, number one fans, and the best support system anyone could ask for.

CONTENTS

Preface vii

Introduction 1

Chapter 1 Never Give Up 5

Chapter 2 Find Your Positives and Stay Humble 14

Chapter 3 The Power of Perspective 28

Chapter 4 Building a Resilient Mindset 42

Chapter 5 Use Your Time Wisely 55

Chapter 6 You're Going to Fail Your Entire Life 66

Chapter 7 Stay Curious 70

Chapter 8 It's Okay to Ask for Help 76

Chapter 9 The Cost of Cheating 83

Chapter 10 Who Cares about Average? 89

Chapter 11 Leave a Positive Timeline 95

Final Message 99

Appendix Facts and Stats about Homeless Students 100

Bibliography 103

PREFACE

"Griffin!"

My grandma stormed into the bedroom where I lay dead asleep, notebook and calculator still in hand. I was exhausted, having spent the last week studying for my advanced placement tests—all *five* of them—that I needed to pass to receive college credit. Not to mention I was still overwhelmed that my dad and I had been evicted from our home just months before my high school graduation.

"*Griffin!*" she shouted again.

My eyes creaked open; the morning birds hadn't even had their worm.

"What, Granny?" I asked, my voice sounding like cracked glass. "What is it?"

"I have someone on the phone that would like to speak to you," she said. I was reluctant but she insisted. "It seems important."

I sat up and grabbed the phone from her. "Hello?"

My cell phone buzzed on the nightstand, and I glanced over, wondering why my phone was blowing up with texts and emails. I heard the person on the other end of the phone talking, but wasn't really processing it.

"I'm sorry, could you repeat that?"

They did and my jaw dropped to the floor. I rushed into the living room, almost knocking over the coffee table, and turned on the TV. A news story headline flashed:

Viral Video: Griffin Furlong
Homeless Valedictorian Set to Graduate.

I looked back at my grandma in disbelief, and in that moment knew my whole life was about to change—forever.

INTRODUCTION

I learned about loss early. After losing my mother to cancer when I was six years old, I watched my father lose his job and almost lose custody of his two children. We lived in countless hotels and motels, and stayed on many friends' couches, and spent our share of nights in homeless shelters. Then just when everything seemed to be getting better, I became homeless again during my senior year of high school.

The National Institute for Children, Poverty, and Homelessness reports that only 64 percent of homeless students graduate from high school. Research also found that unhoused students are 87 percent more likely to drop out of school than their housed peers.

Considering those odds, I wasn't supposed to be valedictorian of my high school class—or even graduate at all, for that matter. It was also unlikely that I'd attend college. And once on campus, there were certainly no guarantees that I'd graduate magna cum laude with a degree in civil engineering. During my college orientation, the counselors said only a handful—unhoused or not—would graduate from the program.

So how did I overcome all the odds stacked against me? Good question. Some people called me a *genius*, some called me *different*. Others called me an *overachiever*. But they had it all wrong; I was no smarter or different than anyone else. However, I did have two things that I owe my progress to.

The first was a better support system than most. I am without question a product of all the helping hands I've had along the way. I spent years of my life being embarrassed to ask for help, whether it was: car rides, food, advice, computer help, or Internet access. There are many people who have influenced my life in the most positive way: teachers, neighbors, friends, and family. You may not have changed the world, but you certainly changed the world for one person and that mattered so much.

The second thing was my mindset. Just because you give someone a fishing pole, doesn't mean they'll catch any fish. So even with the help from others, the only person who got me through each obstacle had to be me. People entered and exited, but they weren't going to learn *for* me, broaden my perspective, or build my mindset. I learned that my mindset was my most important asset. It controlled my attitude, thoughts, actions, priorities, and values. It guided everything about how I lived and operated. I had every excuse to be defeated, to give up, and to allow my environment to control my choices. But I didn't want to be another lost statistic in a research study.

I continuously observed the world around me and made a choice to do better. I slammed the restart button. I wasn't going to live in a shelter my entire life or continue the cycle of poverty. I was going to find a way out and live to talk about it.

I failed many times along the way too. Nothing came easy and nothing was handed to me. I failed quizzes, I failed assignments, I failed my friends. I still fail, and I even fail today. But what separates me from others is that I used those failures to make a conscious decision to be better the next time around.

After observing others in my classrooms for many years, there were always a handful of students who had no passion, no motivation, or no fire to do anything. They were fine with taking naps during class, disrupting the classroom, skipping class, and failing. What I found especially frustrating was that many had a wonderful house, the latest phone, new car, top-tier computer, both parents, and a bed to call their own. They had everything I grew up dreaming about having one day. But for some reason their priorities were misaligned.

Fortunately, observing the other side didn't make me bitter; it inspired me to prove that I didn't need all those things to learn and grow. I wrote this book to serve as a testament that if you have the right mindset, you can accomplish anything no matter the obstacles, lack of resources, or odds against you.

In the first chapters of the book I share stories from my childhood, so you can lace up and walk in my shoes to see what homelessness looked like through my lens. Homeless students face many practical concerns and obstacles trying to balance school with life outside of the classroom like knowing where you'll be sleeping and where your next meal will come from.

There are also emotional challenges: That sick feeling of uncertainty, the lack of progress, and the endless cycle of instability; the fear of not making it out, of never being noticed, of continuing that destructive cycle. Within each story lies a lesson, and questions are posed to help get your brain churning to help spark your curiosity. Whether an experience is destructive or constructive comes down to mindset. My goal is to shed light on the importance of developing a strong mindset and how it can be used to navigate through whatever deep, dark tunnel we might face.

Another goal is to shed light on homelessness to those who don't know what it's like. I am extending an invitation to walk in the shoes, to peek through the lens, and to open the gates to the mind of the homeless valedictorian. I spent years in the classroom listening to students, listening to their parents. I often saw my peers take their luxuries for granted. Let my story be a reminder to treat your luxuries with respect because they could disappear in a flash, just like mine did.

In the remaining chapters I offer lessons learned in school—a list of major principles I developed after stumbling through managing grades, conquering tests, and dealing with peer pressure and social status, and more—and illustrate how they transcend the classroom and apply to larger themes in life.

If there is anything I have learned along the way, it is how to navigate through the trivial and to conquer challenges. Everything I did in my school career paid dividends toward my future. I cannot stress enough the importance of building a foundation. Whether you love or hate school, it can be a great steppingstone to a brighter future—at least that's what it did for me.

Learning is the most important factor, anyway, not the school, as I'll discuss later in this book. If you want to do anything, you have to learn to do *something*. Learning is a perpetual process needed for growth, long after you leave school.

Whether you live in a homeless shelter, have only one parent, or are blessed to have everything you need in life it's never too early to start building the foundational blocks needed to grow. No matter what obstacle you face or what lies ahead, you can accomplish anything you put your mind to.

Let this book serve as a guide. Use it for a reference or for daily motivation to help you unlock the potential you might not even know you have. If I can inspire one person, this book will have fulfilled its purpose. If a poor kid from the homeless shelter can do it, I believe you can too.

CHAPTER 1

NEVER
GIVE UP

*It does not matter how slowly you go, as long
as you do not stop.*
~ Confucius

My mother was five months pregnant with me when doctors diagnosed her with chronic myelogenous leukemia in December 1995. Then two weeks after that my father's dad died, who he had been very close to. I think that double hit laid the foundation for his eventual emotional hurdle, which he later described as a sense of grief, paranoia, and helplessness because things were happening that he had no control over. He and my mom later went to grief counseling for handling terminal illness although I don't know how much it helped in the end.

After I was born my mom received a bone-marrow transplant. She developed graft-versus-host disease, which causes inflammation in different organs. It happened because white blood cells in the donor bone marrow saw my mom's cells as "foreign." So the new bone marrow made antibodies that attacked her skin and organs. At one point she was on more than thirty different medications. But she did go into remission, and life went on although with some changes.

My dad had begun his career in 1987 as a distribution manager at Transwestern Publishing, which was an independent *Yellow Pages* company. He stayed there until 1994 when he started working for a long-term care insurance company, selling insurance for assisted living, which required a lot of travel. But after my mom's diagnosis, my dad wanted to be home for his wife and kids, so he transitioned to car sales at a local Toyota dealership in Louisville, Kentucky. My mother had worked for Porter Paint, doing interior design for homes.

Then in 2000, my mom had a bad fall. My older brother Sean, who was only eight, called my dad who immediately left work to rush home and take my mom to the emergency room. The very next day he was fired for leaving work early. Can you believe someone can get fired for making sure their terminally ill partner wasn't dead? In order to keep his family afloat, he had to find a job at another local car dealer. During this time my parents were open to Sean and me about my mom's illness. Every morning we had a ritual of family hugs before we went to school.

A year later my dad woke up in the middle of the night to screams roaring from outside of the house. It was my mom. He found her lying on our gravel driveway, with her head busted open and blood everywhere. The medications had taken control of her body, which caused her to sleepwalk. That event started a long hospital stay. She had suffered a brain contusion and for a time was supported by a breathing apparatus that was tied into her neck. During that time she couldn't speak, but she was coherent and could write. She knew her time was coming to an end but kept a positive attitude and wrote journal entries about how proud and hopeful she was of Sean and me.

My brother and I went to the hospital and visited her many times. After they removed the respirator, I'd lay with her in the hospital bed while she read books to me. My mom was hospitalized for ten months before doctors let her come home. But by then her body was shutting down.

A few days later on November 1, 2002, my brother and I gave our mom hugs and kisses before leaving for school. After we left, it was only a couple hours later that my mom told my dad she wasn't feeling right, and her body began to seize. He called 911 and an ambulance rushed them both to the hospital. When we left for school that morning, we had no idea that those would be our last hugs and kisses from the person that brought us into this world.

After my mom's funeral, Sean and I shared a moment that I'll never forget. We sat on the floor of our bedroom, tears in our eyes, hoping all of it was just a dream. We hoped we would wake up, and she would be there. But unfortunately we learned that life didn't work that way. After we couldn't produce another tear, we looked each other in the eyes and made a pact to never give up, no matter the obstacles ahead. Sunshine lit the room, and that's when I knew she was there watching over us.

For a while we hung on financially. My parents had never owned a home; they just rented the house I grew up in. So there was no equity, and my mom's illness, even with insurance, had drained my parents' savings and retirement accounts—not to mention there were family complications over visitation rights and custody, so the attorney fees added up. We lived in my childhood home until March 2003, when we moved to an apartment complex a few blocks away, meaning we could stay in the same school. My dad also signed my brother and me up for Little League. He thought it would be good to keep us busy. It became a passion of mine, and I would play every year after that.

One day on the way to practice, our van died right in the middle of an intersection. My dad couldn't afford the repairs or another car, so after that we were stuck for years having to get around mostly on foot or by bus or by sometimes asking for rides from friends and family.

It was a four-mile round trip to the grocery store if you walked along the railroad tracks. Taking surface streets took a half-hour longer each way. What kept me going was love for my dad. He was willing to walk those miles to get groceries to feed his children despite having pinched nerves and a bad back from a horrible car accident he'd been in years prior. If he could do it, I could do it.

Walking those round trips for groceries I learned patience and humility. When cars passed me on the street, I was nervous my friends or peers from school would see me. And many did because they brought it up at school. It was so embarrassing and made me never want to walk anywhere.

I wasn't perfect; many times I turned down my dad. But he kept pushing. He didn't give up. The inevitable was that in order to survive, we needed food. In order to get food, we had limited options, which included walking miles.

In order for my dad to retain custody over his two sons, he had to walk a seven-mile round trip to the courthouse. Regardless of the distance, not having transportation didn't hold him back. He told me that it was the only way. He was going to fight for what he loved, and there was never going to be anything that came between us.

We lived at the apartment for about a year then we moved into a duplex. Around that time my dad left the auto dealership because he wanted to be a stay-at-home parent to his two young, grieving children. So he filed for Social Security survivor benefits and unemployment. From his point of view, he felt obligated to watch after his children and felt he couldn't trust family or friends for help.

The eviction notice stuck out like a sore thumb on the front door of our rental duplex. My dad's desire to be home for us, while good intentioned, started us on the path to homelessness once his unemployment benefits ran out.

We had a week to move out so we stored some of our belongings and everything else went to my maternal grandmother's. The last day we moved our final belongings; it was time to leave my fifty-square-foot attic of a bedroom. My dad, brother, and I began walking, again along the train tracks. We ended up at a picnic bench in a local park. By then it was dark. I looked up to the stars, silently crying for help, hoping someone was listening.

For a while we were nomads, bouncing between friend's couches, my maternal grandmother's home, and hotels. We once asked a church for shelter but they turned us away, so we ended up panhandling for money to stay in a hotel. All I could think about was the free hotel breakfast in the morning.

An old Ramada Inn was our home for a couple weeks. But my family was in desperate need of a saving grace. We were down to our last few dollars, which meant that we couldn't afford the hotel much longer. It felt like another eviction day was approaching, with no idea where our next stop would be.

It turned out to be the Wayside Christian Mission, a homeless shelter in the heart of downtown Louisville. (Ironically, the building now houses a five-star restaurant.). The first day there I was greeted by two bunk beds in a two-hundred-square-foot room. In the back right corner was a shared bathroom with no mirror. There was no heat, no hot water, and the shower was covered in mold. The stench reminded me of a mix between rotten mildew and old diapers. I remember how the worn wooden floors creaked with every step. The mattresses were thin and made of a hard, bright-green plastic, and that initial night my family didn't have sheets.

There was already a family occupying the right bunk bed, which meant my family had the left bunk. That night it was impossible to sleep; you could hear the rats living under the wooden floors squealing and the other family's snoring. Plus I was nervous about my future, embarrassed by my butchered haircut and not having many clothes, and anxious at the thought of kids at school finding out where we were living. Keeping my situation a secret at school would be very stressful. But despite all that I was still thankful because I had my family by my side, a roof over my head, and food from the soup kitchen so we wouldn't go hungry.

A few months into our stay at Wayside, my dad signed me up to play Little League baseball late in the season. My team was winless with a 0–6 record. The shelter provided me with an old, thirteen-inch softball glove. It had a huge pouch of a web, which made sense—if I was playing *softball*. To play middle infield it was about four inches larger than it needed to be. I was also provided a pair of used cleats and pants that were a size too big. Lastly, I found a dusty, old cap in the bin.

My dad looked at me and said, "Well, it ain't gonna be the equipment that plays good ball."

And I couldn't argue because he was right; I was going to have to make it work. Before practice, I got a sharpie at the shelter's front desk and wrote *Never Give Up* under the bill of the cap.

After I joined the team, we won twelve straight games and went on to play in the championship game. The other coaches in the league selected me as an all-star, with the first overall pick. And during that entire season, only one teammate knew I was homeless.

The power of those three little words on my cap. When life throws you curveballs, it's important to remind yourself of why you step up to the plate to begin with. The next time you walk into the batter's box, play your theme music, and prepare for the challenge at hand. Just because a curveball is hard to hit sometimes, don't give up; step back up to the plate.

It's never too late to build this mindset, even if you do strike out looking. At least you're at the plate trying. That takes a lot more courage than someone that never wants another at bat. We fail our minds when we choose to not step up to the plate again. Just remember that giving up is too easy. In order to grow, we need to be tested. In order to maintain that consistent growth, we simply can never give up.

The baseball analogy is apt because the lessons learned from the sport can be applied to life. Unlike some sports, baseball allows you a unique opportunity. There is no time limit, you typically get at least three chances to bat, and during every pitch anything can happen. You have to make the most of each opportunity. If you give up on any play, you let your whole team down. That one moment matters.

Also, baseball helped me build a resilient mindset. The number one thing that got me through all of life's curveballs was the mindset to never give up. I wrote those words under every cap, every season. I still have the box of baseball caps sitting in my closet to remind myself every day of the struggle, of where I had come from, of the lack of equipment I had, and of the hoops I had to hurdle.

As one of my favorite artists, Jermaine Cole, once said: *There's beauty in the struggle.* The beauty was that the struggle reminded me that I always had the eye to hit curveballs, over again and again. Of course, that awareness and mindset took a while to develop, so as a kid life often seemed overwhelmingly cruel.

For my fifth-grade graduation, there were no school buses operating that day so my dad and I had looked up the metro bus schedule and mapped out the best route to school. The next morning we got up at 6:00 a.m. sharp, got dressed, then began our thirty-minute walk to the bus stop. We took two buses then had a half-hour walk to the graduation—in the hot June summer. My friends and peers passed us by in their cars.

When I got to graduation, I received many odd looks. My dad and I were sweaty, and I was underdressed. Everyone else was clean cut with nice business casual clothes while I wore a long sleeve cotton polo shirt one size too big, jeans, and tennis shoes. I remember feeling embarrassed, with lumps in my chest. I didn't want to show my face. I had never felt like more of an outcast and asked my dad why we even came.

Truth was I felt like an outcast every single day of fifth grade because I rode a special bus from the homeless shelter that looked different from all of the other buses. My brother and I had to wake up two hours earlier than normal to walk a mile to the special bus stop that served the homeless kids or else we'd miss school. Since Sean was already in middle school, I was the only kid to hop off that bus at my elementary school, and all the other students at school had a front row seat to the show.

Kids asked questions left and right. *Where do you live? Where does that bus go?*

I always answered that I lived close to downtown then tried to change the subject because I didn't want the other students knowing I lived in the homeless shelter. That wouldn't have been *cool,* so it was difficult being honest and truthful. Every day I would wait fifteen minutes after school ended to leave so no one could see me get on that bus. This may not seem like a big deal, but it was traumatic to me because it made me feel different, like I didn't belong.

Life had gotten progressively worse for me over the span of my childhood. A nice house turned into an apartment. The apartment turned into friends' couches. The friends' couches turned into hotels, and the hotels became homeless shelters. But there's a limit for how long you can stay in a shelter, and we reached that limit twice.

Little did I know at the time, but all it was all a test of stamina and patience. Reflecting back now, I realize that it prepared me for an opportunity I'd need grit for. Don't give up right before this opportunity presents itself.

My opportunity presented itself after the five-year marathon of loss, homelessness, poverty, and almost losing my father in a custody battle. Finally, my family was blessed with a glimmer of light.

SUMMARY

- It does not matter how slowly you go, as long as you do not stop.

CHAPTER 2

FIND YOUR POSITIVES
AND STAY HUMBLE

Stay true in the dark and humble in the spotlight.
~Harold B. Lee

I will never forget the day.

We'd been kicked out of our second homeless shelter and ended up collecting enough money for two nights at the nearby Best Western. We were on our last dime. Then our cheap Nokia Tracfone rang; it was my dad's mom. She lived in Jacksonville, Florida, with my aunt and uncle and announced that she was coming to come pick us up—a twenty-two-hour round trip for her.

Between the Social Security benefits and some money from my grandma's savings, we would be able to rent a small, five-hundred-square-foot house in Jacksonville. Sean and I jumped for joy then sprinted to the hotel lobby and began Googling what schools we'd go to. We talked about how we would play sports, focus on school, and hit the reset button.

Fast forward to Florida. Things were better, but I wouldn't say all our problems were solved. My dad was still battling mental and physical health obstacles, which made it hard for him to keep a job. We had limited transportation, no Internet access, and we lived far enough away from school and the grocery store to make it a stretch.

However, our situation was still twenty steps forward from being in a homeless shelter. Moving into that rental property was like moving into a mansion. And even though we still had to walk to the grocery store, borrow money from my grandma, and live on government aid, we found our positives. More importantly, we hadn't given up, and we kept going regardless of how long it took to get an opportunity to see some light.

You Won't Go to College if You Go to That High School

As a thirteen-year-old in middle school, I had to decide which high school I was going to go to. I attended open houses for the top two nationally ranked high schools. They were rivals, so the pitch of each school was: *We're better than the other school, so come here.* I wasn't sold, but many of my peers and their parents thought it was gold.

What was going through my head was: *Do I really want to go to a school where every single person is the best of the best? How do you stand out? What happens if I fail out of the first year?* From my point of view, the last thing I could afford was failing out of school. I wouldn't say I was intimidated or scared, I'm sure I would have been fine, but I had to think logically about a long-term plan for my future.

The open house hammered that they were going to prepare you for college, hence the word *preparatory* in the school's name. Some of my friends, and even family, were adamant about me going there, and I saw the disappointment on their faces when I chose the nearby First Coast High School, the F-rated school in Duval County.

First, that was Sean's high school, and he had built a small legacy there, which I believed would help me jump-start my relationship with the teachers and coaches. My main priorities were academics and baseball, so I wanted the best chance to create those relationships quickly. I also loved how big the campus was and how close it was to home—keep in mind we had no car and very little money. I loved the Friday night football game under the lights; it almost felt like I was attending a small college game. I also loved and valued its diversity because that's how the actual world is. Diversity introduces you to more perspectives, which I believe has its own special value.

I chose First Coast even though people warned me not to because it wouldn't set me up for college. As if the school takes the tests, spends hours studying, learns, and applies to college. I wanted to prove their theory wrong. It doesn't matter what school you went to. School is a means to an end; it provides you with an opportunity, and it's up to each individual to make the most of that opportunity. As a society we love labels and awards, and the other preparatory schools had plenty. But what matters is the hard work, dedication, and sacrifice of the individual student, regardless of the school.

At some point in a student's career, they will need to make a choice of acting on their priorities rather than having a system, parents, or anyone else making them on their behalf.

My dad never had to tell me to do homework, study for a test, or read because I made the choice extremely early on when I was nine years old that learning was a way out of poverty. I wanted to learn, so I showed up to class, I asked questions, and I studied. If you're ready to make the choice of taking action in your priorities, it will never matter what school, company, or brand you choose. Life is the best school; you'll learn many things along the way.

Regardless of what other people thought, I had to remind myself to count my positives and stay humble, even when more obstacles peeked around the corner.

Is the U-Haul Half Empty or Half Full?

I was four months away from my high school graduation and was getting a ride home from my girlfriend and her family. As we pulled up into the rocky driveway, I noticed a U-Haul truck in front of our pale-green rental house.

"Are you moving?" my girlfriend's mom asked.

"Not that I know of," I replied with a lump in my throat.

My dad walked out of the house with two strangers who loaded my dresser and bed into the back of the truck, joining almost all of our other belongings that had already been packed.

"Looks like you are moving," said my girlfriend's brother.

I got out of the car, dreading to walk up to the patio. My dad appeared at the front door.

"Griff, I'm sorry bud. We'll figure everything out."

I was in utter shock and had no words, just a cold, familiar feeling I thought I'd left behind in Louisville. I didn't know we were behind on rent. Images of the homeless shelters, the cafeteria food, the plastic mattresses, and the shared family bunk beds filled my head. As did the question of where I would sleep? Where would my dad go?

Sean was away at college and I'd find out that was one reason we lost the rental. Between no longer receiving his Social Security survivor benefit and my grandma finally depleting all her savings in helping us, we'd run out of money. And I didn't work, considering high school my full-time job. Just when you thought everything was becoming more normal, here we were, homeless again.

The idea of asking my girlfriend's mom if I could stay the night with them for a while made me sick to my stomach. But that was the only thing I could do, no matter how embarrassing. I needed a place to sleep, to study, to prepare for college. Luckily, her family accepted me into their home, more than I could have ever imagined. But I was still thrown for an emotional loop. What about my dad? I was going to college soon and was nervous that he wouldn't have a safe place to live while I moved two hours away.

I had a choice to make. I could either cry about it and let this setback torpedo everything I'd worked so hard for at school, or I could not give up and finish strong, which I did but it was easier said than done.

In that moment of uncertainty, I had to settle my brain and remind myself of the positives in my life. I was healthy, I was loved, I was on the verge of college, and thanks to my girlfriend's family I would have a roof over my head. Her family kept me positive, made me feel at home, and fed me. Once again I became the product of helping hands through generous acts of kindness.

The night of the U-Haul fiasco, I borrowed my girlfriend's computer and began writing a speech, an inspirational message to any of the students I'd ever crossed paths with. It was everything I had always wanted to share, and it came from the heart.

I thought: *Wouldn't this be a great plot to a story?* I was the author of my own life. My keystrokes were my actions. And my actions were dictated from the strength and consistency of my mindset. In under an hour, I had a whole speech, with some of the main messages being: Don't dwell on the past; use it as motivation toward your future. Do not live a life without purpose. Never give up.

This ultimately became my high school valedictorian speech to the Class of 2014. I hadn't even been officially declared the valedictorian yet by the school; I still had to finish the last semester with all As to make it stand. I believed that all this was supposed to happen, that my purpose was to share my story in hopes that it could inspire others. And so I grabbed hold of that vision of delivering this inspirational message to my class—and to you. The next time you find yourself on one of life's difficult paths, pause and take a moment. Smile and look around. Find your positives.

Find the glass—or the U-Haul— half full, like I did.

Ivy League or Bust

During my last semester as a senior I again was faced with the decision of what school to attend next. I applied to more than fifty colleges because why not? And also because my brother called me every single day telling me to apply. The more schools I had on my list, the better the probability of acceptance and scholarship opportunities. Many colleges offered high school valedictorians free rides, so I tried my best to scope it out. I was lucky enough to get interviewed to attend Duke University, the Ivy League of the South. Vanderbilt University was also on the list. I even applied to a real Ivy League school, Dartmouth.

After months of applications, interviews, and tours, I finally chose my college. I had been set on this college the entire time in high school. When I told people I was staying local to attend Florida State University, which was a two-and-a-half-hour drive from Jacksonville, I got pretty mixed reactions, the majority being confusion.

Valedictorian?

Florida State?

The party school with the football team?

Yikes.

It was the same thing I had faced in high school, with people telling me I wouldn't make it because I'd chosen the wrong school. That I was making a bad decision. I was missing good opportunities.

I understood the critics. Having a brand name university on your resume can speak volumes. I'm sure the alumni base of Ivy League schools is outstanding, with many connections and opportunities. But I wanted to prove this idea that your school is what matters most was misguided. It was less about proving the critics wrong and more about proving to myself that I could accomplish anything, regardless of the school.

I never liked brands anyway. I never needed a brand to make myself feel better. Besides, most brand names were expensive. And the same goes for these Ivy League schools. Unfortunately I wasn't receiving much of a scholarship offer from those schools either. So the choice of choosing $100,000 of debt after school or being debt-free became an easy choice.

Four and a half years later, my time at Florida State University came to an end. It took me an extra half year because engineering generally takes longer. It was the best experience of my life. I made some of the greatest, lifelong friends. I made connections. I came out of college debt-free. School paid me. I graduated magna cum laude with a bachelor of science in civil engineering. Not too many people get to say that!

I studied the same topics as the brilliant minds of our past, for free. I learned the same thing any Harvard or Vanderbilt physics student did because learning isn't based on the school; it's based on the individual. If you want to learn something badly enough, you will seek the answers.

The moral here is never let anyone else's perspective overshadow what you want in life. It's okay to do what's best for you and what you enjoy. Turn the negativity into positivity. Whether you end up attending a community college, technical college, a no-name school, or even dropping out and creating your own business, as long as you have a plan and broaden your perspective, you can do anything. It's your future and your story that you're writing. Your growth is dependent on *you* and never the school, company, or anything else. School is just a place; learning is an everlasting, perpetual motion machine to get yourself where you want to be.

No One Cares, Do Better

Fear of failure can motivate you to your absolute best performance.
~ Jon S. Rennie, *All in the Same Boat*

A month after I went homeless in high school, I was sitting in my second period class when I was invited to the guidance counselor's office. She announced that I was valedictorian of my class. I felt a mix of emotions, more positive than anything. I immediately called my brother and told him the news.

At the time, he was dating a news producer for the local First Coast news station, and he told her all about my situation. She was adamant about compiling a news story because she thought it could help with scholarships and college acceptances. She offered to send a cameraman over to the high school to film me. I was initially reluctant because the last thing I wanted was for everyone to know about my situation. I was embarrassed to share. But she was persistent so I finally agreed.

After school I met with the cameraman, and we filmed a few shots in front of my high school. My peers were hanging around in the background, confused.

What's going on? Why are you being filmed?

I shrugged and smiled awkwardly. I didn't have an answer for them because I didn't know what I was doing.

Prior to the story airing on the local station, I was nervous because of the vulnerability, even if only a few people watched it. The news producer calmed me down the night before the release.

"Don't worry, Griff. It's gonna air in the early morning when no one watches."

Within a matter of days, I went viral on every major news outlet in America. I woke up to millions of views, emails, and text messages. People from around the world reached out.

So a month before college I went on a cross-country media tour, appearing on *Good Morning America* with Robin Roberts, the *NBC Nightly News* with Ann Curry, and even doing interviews with *Sports Illustrated*. I traveled from New York to Los Angeles—and several places in between—sharing my experiences.

I ate dinner at Nobu with a couple hundred dollars actress Keke Palmer gave to me. A friend created a GoFundMe account linked to my name that raised more than $100,000 to help support not only my college endeavors but also my family's financial future.

That was also the summer of the American Legion World Series, where I played baseball in a nationally televised baseball tournament on ESPN, which took place in front of 10,000 fans. My face seemed to be everywhere.

I'll admit, it was heady stuff.

So on the heels of all this hype I stepped into college and promptly failed my first assignment. It was a chemistry lab report. I had butchered the entire report formatting. *How inspirational*, I thought, *to achieve something so great and to have such a good message to share then fail myself right out of college.* I suffered the ultimate low in my school career. I was mortified and never told anyone about that, not even my family or friends, because my pride was taken away.

In hindsight it was great that I felt that way because it meant I cared. Deeply. That emotional response presented a decision: either give up and let that grade dictate what college was going to be for me or do something about that failing grade and make sure it didn't happen again.

Because of our family struggles, I had learned early in life that failure was an opportunity. So I made the choice to do something about it. I immediately set up a meeting with my professor and walked through the entire report from start to finish, discussing how I could improve for the next time. I ended up with an A in the class and most importantly, I didn't let it derail my entire college career or devalue who I was as a person. All it took was a choice and action.

When I was a sophomore in college, I landed an internship at a Fortune 100 company. I was young and inexperienced but eager to learn.

I was fortunate enough to work there for three straight summers, and as my college graduation approached, anticipated getting a job offer from the company. But eventually I was informed no offer was coming.

After work I took a five-mile walk along the beach and reflected. It was one of the few times in my life where I wasn't picked. Whether it had been baseball, basketball, or school plays, I had been chosen to join the team. But this time I didn't make the cut; I was told I needed to work on leadership, communication, and organization.

Again, I had a couple of choices: I could be sad or light a fire under myself. I looked inward and thought: *Okay, I guess I need to do better then.* Rather than blowing off the constructive criticism I had received, I used it as motivation to work on myself and make sure I'd get the next job.

I needed leadership skills, so I became the project manager for my senior design project. I made sure my team was always on track, and we ended up orchestrating a great project and presentation.

I needed communication skills, so I began reading more books, talking to more students, and participating in more public speaking events. I even researched and worked on my email writing skills, keeping the messages concise and clear.

I needed better organization, so I developed a process for documenting my computer files and notes. I also made it a habit to always keep my desk organized and my room clean. Orderly environment, orderly mind.

When I graduated from college, I brought those principles I had worked so hard on developing that last semester to my new job. I spent countless hours learning the job inside and out. In a couple of years, I worked my way up to a role that a twenty-four-year-old at the time shouldn't have been doing. But it was those foundational building blocks that got me there. It was also about never giving up and using constructive criticism to my advantage. I was coachable, teachable, and I didn't get defensive.

Most importantly, I had to remind myself to find my positives and stay humble. Who was I to complain? I wasn't in the shelter anymore. I had the luxury of living in a condo a few steps away from the beach during my internship, which paid me a very competitive wage. I had the time of my life, made lifelong friends, and was in overall great health. I soon realized that my positives outweighed my negatives. Searching for the brighter side allowed me to combat negativity and build humility, and it could help do the same for you. Next time you're feeling defeated, remind yourself of everything you're thankful for.

How Much a Dollar Cost?

In my sophomore year of college, I was walking back from my best friend Michael's apartment. It was a late night and along East Tennessee Street there were always large groups of homeless people. As I approached one of the gas stations, a tall, lanky Black man emerged from the shadows and approached me.

The first thing that came to mind was wondering what excuse I could make not to give him money.

"I don't mean to be a bother to you, young man, but I'm really hungry. Could you spare some change?" the homeless man asked.

All I had was a $20 bill in my pocket, and I was not prepared to spend all of it.

"I'll be right back," I told him.
It was clear by his expression that he thought I was making an excuse.
Inside the gas station, I grabbed water, snacks, and asked for small bills back when I checked out. When I walked out of the gas station, the man was gone. I did not want to spend my time helping this man; I just wanted to be home safe in my bed, which made me feel guilty.

I found the man lying on a piece of cardboard in the dark away from the building. He was in rougher shape than I thought. I reluctantly walked over.

"Excuse me, sir. I got you some water and snacks."

I opened the bag and held them out. He looked at me and smiled.

I cracked a smile back. "My name is Griffin, sir. I hope this helps you tonight."

"You're the first person to look me in the eyes today," he said, his eyes tearing. "I lost my job after the 2008 market crash and haven't been the same since. I don't do drugs or drink alcohol. I smoke a couple packs of cigarettes a week, but I'm not a bad person."

I was no longer worried about getting home. That was just an excuse I had told myself. He opened up about his life and the job he'd had. He was also from Kentucky, had no immediate family, and was trying to save enough money for a bus ticket back to Kentucky and get back to work.

"It's harder than it seems when you have nothing. People like you have support from your families, so never take that for granted," he said.

How the roles had turned. He began offering his perspective of me, telling me how my life was, based on what he was seeing on the outside. I had a nice Fossil watch on, which I had bought 75 percent off from a close-out sale. I had a Ralph Lauren polo shirt I got at Plato's Closet for $5.

I didn't blame him for making his judgment; we were both wrong that night. To him I was another preppy, rich white boy with daddy's money to spare. To me he was another homeless Black man on the street.

I politely refuted his vision of me as misguided and told him a year earlier I had been homeless. As I told him about losing my mom to leukemia, the financial struggles, going in and out of homeless shelters—all the rock bottom moments of my life—his eyes opened wide. I told him that throughout high school I worked my butt off to get noticed because school was my only way out, and I was fortunate to get a full ride scholarship.

The eyes—not the clothes on your back—are a portal to a man's soul.

He was as proud as a dad hearing good news from his son. He told me to keep going because special things were ahead. He offered to pray with me if I didn't mind. I accepted.

It was a beautiful moment in my life. Two opposites connecting in the world. Didn't matter what skin color, what background, or where we were headed. All that mattered was that moment in time. We shared a connection that will stay ingrained with me forever. I couldn't help but wonder: *Was it God himself?*

It reminded me of that Kendrick Lamar song "How Much a Dollar Cost?" that came out only a few weeks before this incident. In Kendrick's story, he struggles with an internal battle of whether he should spare money for a homeless beggar on the street, vacillating between resentment and guilt. All the homeless man wanted was a dollar, but in the end Kendrick refused because his perspective was that the man would just buy crack with it. At the end of the story, the homeless man is revealed to be the Holy Spirit and not giving the dollar cost Kendrick a spot in Heaven.

It seems like the world throws me into situations as a test. And sometimes those tests feel way too good to be true due to the nature of the lesson. The tests come down to a choice. The beauty of it is that I always have the power of choice. I believe there is no right or wrong choice, just a choice that can only do good in the world.

That night I had a few choices: outright ignore the man; tell him to piss off and get a job; hand him a $1 bill; or have a conversation with him. Who was I, the motivational homeless valedictorian gifted over $100,000, to turn down a homeless man asking for a dollar on the street? I wanted to touch the world. I wanted to travel everywhere and reach out to all the homeless people in America. I wanted to start a TV show, a movie, and a book to help start a business that helps homeless people get on track. Mr. Motivational, trying to change the world with one word at a time. That was my vision, and I couldn't even spare a homeless man a couple of dollars?

I certainly learned that you have to be humbled to be humble. We all just want to be noticed. We all yearn for love. Not all of us are lazy. Sometimes we just need that glimpse of hope, which can come from the people around us. People are books waiting to be read. You never know if that one conversation could change the rest of your life, or theirs.

SUMMARY

- When adversity strikes, continue to find your positives, and stay humble.

CHAPTER 3

THE POWER
OF PERSPECTIVE

People are books waiting to be read.
~ Unknown

Perspective is our point of view, our attitude, and our way of thinking about anything. Shaping your outlook on life ultimately shapes the way you live your life. I'm not here to dictate how you should think, feel, or act. But what I can tell you is that I discovered a way to consistently grow my perspective, which impacted my life for the better.

Everyone has a story to tell. And everyone is writing their story through their actions every day. But within our individual stories is one that's larger than us. Sharing stories can help expand our perspective but only if we are willing to see through their eyes and feel through their heart.

Being rich, poor, blue, red, alabaster, or ebony can divide us if we blindly believe what we hear from others including our parents, friends, social media, and propaganda passing itself off as fair and balanced news.

When we fail to take the initiative and look at things objectively, ask questions, and actually listen, we end up with a one-dimensional, narrow-minded perspective. That translates to picking sides and too often drawing a line between *you* and *me* instead of reaching across to create an *us*. I grew my perspective by becoming an investigative journalist.

The Investigative Journalist

The first step in building perspective is to be an investigative journalist. Before you develop a way of thinking, believe something to be true, or form an opinion of someone, you need to research the facts, ask questions, and come up with your own conclusions to base your opinion on. This will not only make the world a better place for you and the people around you, but it will also open new doors of opportunity.

Facts matter. Imagine being that person who shares an inaccurate or untrue story. Imagine using a fake source as your best source for your argument. Imagine developing a perspective of someone based on false information. Imagine never getting to know someone because of your false assumptions, fake facts, unreliable sources, or unreasonable perspectives that clouded your judgment.

You have a right to an opinion, but that opinion may change if you allow yourself to view it from another perspective. Approaching the world like an investigative journalist could potentially change your life.

When I lived in the homeless shelter, I discovered that the perspective of the little boy I shared a room with was quite different from mine. For one thing he was Black and I was White. He had lived in Section Eight housing before they came to the shelter. We'd lived in a nice house in a great neighborhood before things turned upside down.

Although we had different upbringings, different skin color, and different slang, once we shared our perspectives we realized we were actually more alike than we were different. I couldn't slip on his shoes or peek through his lens until I asked questions and listened to his stories.

Our willingness to share wiped the fog from our clouded lens. And we ultimately built a strong relationship during those tough times in our lives.

Right now you may have a perception of homeless people. In fact, research shows that the term *homeless* carries a near-universal negative connotation, which is why you'll now hear the term *unhoused* used. So let me share my perspective from once being a young, homeless student.

What Does Homelessness Look Like?

That depends on who you ask.

If you ask me, homelessness is a never-ending cycle of uncertainty. When you're homeless, it's difficult to measure progress because progress doesn't ever seem to happen. Day after day, the hole you're in seems to get deeper and deeper, and you start questioning when change is going to happen. So you end up losing large amounts of confidence, which in turn causes you to eventually lose your sense of purpose and belonging to the world.

Every night in the homeless shelter I thought: *When will we ever get out of here? Does anyone even care?* I had to rely on my dreams to escape the reality I was living.

Just when we thought we had saved enough money, it had to be spent. Just when we thought my dad had landed a job, there was no more job. Just when we thought we were taking a step forward, it was two steps back.

So why even take a step forward? Why even do anything at all? Nothing we did seemed to make a difference—or to matter.

That type of mindset can create a destructive cycle that undermines a family's future and ability to find permanent housing security. That is exactly how the cycle of homelessness and poverty continues. If the children choose not to care and choose to give up, they have a higher chance of continuing that forward into the future.

If you ask some other people, the solution to homelessness is easy. *Just go get a job* or *Just do this.* According to some of my peers' parents I heard growing up, people on food stamps were lazy and stealing from the government. Everything is so easy; you just press a button and a good paying job and a house you can afford magically happens.

I listened to these kinds of opinions about the homeless and poor and held my tongue. Many were unaware that I was poor, and it brought out the ugly truth of their perspective. This was what they truly thought of me.

If only they knew...

The Reality

My family wasn't lazy. And we weren't stealing from the government. Federal aid kept us alive and gave us an opportunity. My dad did apply for jobs, which was top on his list besides making sure he didn't lose his boys. But no one saw it from his perspective. No one ever felt the way he did when he lost the woman he loved who was his support, his partner, and his coparent. No one saw the miles he walked to keep us fed, secure, and safe. No one saw the countless hours I spent behind closed doors studying.

Lazy? Far from it.

When you have Internet access, a phone, a car, a computer, a roof over your head, income, a savings account, nourishment, and a family that can help, it puts you one step ahead of people who don't have any of those luxuries. Each and every one of those items cost time, effort, and money and provides a special security blanket that makes you feel warm and cozy. Your only problems are first-world problems, like your phone being too slow or not knowing what designer sneakers you want to get next. Money provides a safety net.

In school I observed the values and priorities of other students. Partying, maintaining social status, getting a new car, and dating the most popular person in school is what often consumed them then. If anyone was aware of how fortunate they were, they didn't indicate it. Nothing was ever enough.

What I struggled to get my hands on, they received with a snap of their fingers. From my perspective there was no excuse for those students not to do well in school or not to take it seriously or want more for themselves. Their eyes were set on different priorities, which was reasonable because high-school status seemed so important at the time. It was cool not to care, to skip class, and to drive the best car. It was cool to be the class clown and make kids laugh. It was cool to be a rebel and not learn. From my perspective, I thought learning and respecting the teachers was cool. I thought it was cool to tutor students, to teach them something new, to learn something and master it myself. I thought it was cool to learn and to grow, especially considering where I came from. It was all I had to make it out of poverty.

At one point in my life, everything had been normal. I lived in a nice neighborhood, I had a Nintendo, I had my own bed, and I had both parents by my side. Then my life changed forever. Because of that I learned the value of humility and how to appreciate the small things.

If you take away anything from this, examine your supporting cast and the luxuries around you and understand their value. Develop an appreciation for what you have because they can be gone in an instant, just like mine were.

One Step Forward, Two Steps Back

There are many common themes during homelessness but the one certainty was for each step forward there were always two steps back. One of the things that kept me trying to move forward was my evolving perspective of the world and life.

Theme 1: Evictions and losing valuable possessions

Evictions and getting kicked off of people's couches are common themes during homelessness. The instability creates a cycle of the question: *what's next?*

Eviction days were always stressful because there was nothing worse than having to move and not having anywhere to go. When you have little money, it becomes difficult to rent a U-Haul so you have to find a way to keep track of all your personal belongings. When the evictions become more and more common, you end up paring down the possessions you hold onto. After a while it feels like nothing belongs to you.

The first time we got evicted, most of our possessions went to a storage facility. Some belongings got thrown away, and some came with us to our next location. Storage units cost money, so once we couldn't afford it any longer, we lost everything: my mother's belongings, pictures, memorable childhood items, school awards, CDs and cassettes, jewelry, etc.

Not only did we lose valuable material possessions, but we lost a piece of our identity. We were once a normal family that gathered in the living room, ate at the dining room table together, and hugged each other goodnight. All those moments and possessions became mere memories. But I learned that the most valuable possessions were not anything that money could buy. What I learned to value the most were my time, relationships, and my attitude.

Theme 2: No Internet or computer access

One day my teacher asked out loud to the class: "Does anyone *not* have Internet access?"

Great, I thought. She should have just asked: *Is anyone poor?* because it felt like the same question. Almost every student had Internet and a computer—at least to my knowledge—except me.

I wasn't strong enough to let anyone know. I didn't want pity and special treatment. So now I had a difficult challenge in front of me: figuring out how to complete my class project because every single aspect was based on Internet research. I couldn't stay late after school either or else I'd miss the bus. My only option was going to the public library. I had to look up the metro bus routes on how to get there. Plus, I lived in a rough part of downtown, so I needed to go in daylight and be cautious of my surroundings.

At the public library, using the printer costs money, which added a hurdle to jump over because if I messed up, I couldn't afford to print. If I couldn't afford to print, then I had no assignment to turn in.

I also had to rely on a USB drive to save files because the documents were deleted from the computer after logging off. But when I got to the library, I realized my USB drive had been left at the shelter. So not only did I waste money, but I also wasted time. Once again, I was trying to take a step forward but it resulted in two steps back.

Some might read our situation and think: *Why didn't your dad just get a job?*

Unfortunately, he was not computer literate. The world had shifted to online applications, and when you don't know how to fill them out, you're two steps behind other job candidates. Also, if you don't have Internet access or a computer to develop computer literacy, you have to: 1) travel to the business to get an application and then 2) travel back for a job interview. We did not have the luxury of hopping into our car. Each and every job had to be close or along the metro bus route. Nothing is as simple as it seems, especially if you don't see through the lens of what other people are going through.

These circumstances made me realize that nothing was ever going to be handed to me. If I needed to solve a problem or get something finished, I had to act. When I was fortunate enough to access the Internet, I developed as much computer literacy as I could so I would never be two steps behind.

Theme 3: Little-to-no transportation.

Think of how easy it is to hop in the car and go to the grocery store, your doctor's appointments, school, and work. When you're homeless, you might not be able to afford a car payment, insurance, gas, and maintenance because there is little-to-no income being generated.

When you're a homeless student athlete, you have to find ways to get to practices and games. You can never develop your own schedule because you're constantly trying to fit into everyone else's. If you're reliant on rides back to the shelter, that means someone you know is going to know where you live, which piles on pressures of embarrassment. I felt like I missed out on huge opportunities, especially with baseball and other extra curriculars. It was all because it was difficult to get from point A to point B.

My perspective of travel evolved, and I would never take it for granted again. Travel was an essential element, and the lack of it had helped me build resiliency. I learned never to be embarrassed of walking or taking public transportation. If I had to be somewhere, I had to try, no matter the distance.

Theme 4: Isolation

When you're homeless, you feel caged in and reliant on others to get you out. Oftentimes at school I was afraid to open up to my teachers and guidance counselors about my situation. It wasn't their fault or mine. A huge part of it was my own embarrassment and insecurity, which I knew I had to overcome.

So despite the feeling of isolation, I sat in class with my thoughts to myself and instead of giving up, I learned how to reflect, evaluate, and create awareness. The world wasn't out to get me. I was out to get the world. And building that positive perspective opened doors for me.

Theme 5: Single, separated, divorced, or widowed parents.

The last time I saw my mom, I was holding her cold hand at her funeral hoping she would wake up. My brother and I lost the woman that brought us into the world, and my dad lost the love of his life, his partner, and his everything. The hardest aspect trying to understand about death as a six-year-old was the concept of eternity. She was gone forever and could never be brought back to the world, and I could never talk to her again. Not only did it put us two steps back mentally but financially, socially, and emotionally as well.

From a parent's perspective, taking care of your children is a job within itself. When you're a single parent, you need extra help to balance work and home life. My dad said his priority was to make sure we were busy with school and sports to keep us distracted from our situation. It was a double-edged sword for him because he wanted to be a stay-at-home, but he also knew he needed to work to be able to provide for us. When you are taking care of a six- and ten-year-old, they can't just be left anywhere without guidance.

My parents played a major role in developing my perspective of love and loss. Unfortunately, my mom never had the opportunity to see me play baseball or graduate, but she taught me how to read. She had kept a diary ever since she was in elementary school and even during her time in the hospital, which I had the fortune of reading.

Though it was sad to read, especially her acceptance that she would never see her two boys grow, I learned that death didn't have to be just darkness. She was optimistic and had a great sense of humor. When she passed, it made me happy thinking of her being in a better place where she always wanted to go and happy as can be. I had the choice to think in that way instead of thinking negatively.

As for love and support, my dad is my number one fan. He believes in me no matter what my interests are—academics, acting, sports, and even this book. One time in middle school, we were able to borrow my grandma's car, so we went to the nearby Little League field. We spent nearly five hours doing batting practice. He encouraged me to hit left-handed, my non-dominant swing, and set a goal that we weren't going to leave until I hit at least one home run, which seemed to be a nearly impossible task. We spent hours, ball after ball, even though his back and shoulders were failing him. But he wanted to accomplish the goal just as much as me. Then finally, with a crack of the bat, the ball soared over the fence. No one else ever saw that side of my dad, only me.

Theme 6: Mental health

When you're between the ages of six and twelve years old, you don't have the cognitive abilities yet to understand the magnitude of mental illness. As I reflect now as a young adult, it's easy to see its impact on daily life. Mental health is like battling an invisible barrier between where you are and where you know you need to go.

When I was growing up, I knew something was different with my dad. I felt the worry in his voice and could sense the paranoia and grief. But I didn't understand until later.

Theme 7: Little-to-no social life.

Homelessness puts you two steps behind in the social world. Sometimes I couldn't keep up with what other kids were talking about; I seemed to be missing something. They were up-to-date with the latest television shows, sports, video games, and news. At the shelter I could occasionally watch movies the nearby church would host, but that was about it.

Sleepovers are a popular thing among children. I never bothered asking any of my classmates to come over to the homeless shelter because why would they? I would avoid spending the night at anyone's house because I knew I'd have to get dropped back off at the homeless shelter.

I recall one moment in fourth grade in particular. There were a few kids in my class that organized a sleepover, and they encouraged me to come. I reluctantly agreed. The next morning the parents offered to take everyone home, so they loaded the troops into the van. I was hoping that I would be the last one dropped off. Unfortunately, I was the first. The parents and the kids were perplexed when I directed them to a nearby hotel. I was bombarded with questions the next day in class, but I was too embarrassed to answer.

There were only two options to get out of misery: end my life or make the most of my time. I thought about those options often, but I always chose the latter. I think what drives people to take the first option sometimes is the lack of a social life, and I don't blame them.

Is that quiet kid in the back of the class doing okay?

Who knows because no one ever cared to figure out.

Social belonging is important because it makes you feel like you matter. If you don't feel like you matter to others, nothing matters to you.

If I just killed myself, no one would care or notice, so why not? Nothing even matters, not my friends, family, school—or me.

At the end of the day, sometimes we just want attention, the good kind of attention, the genuine kind. Less invisibility and more acknowledgement. More voices and ears open to be heard.

I developed the perspective that the world was full of opportunities. Things get bad along the way, but there was always a choice to make it a little better. I have this one life, and it never made sense to waste it.

With each challenge you face, there may be one step forward and two steps back. But regardless of the direction the steps take, keep your eyes looking forward and never back. You'll discover that when you have a vision, you'll always have a direction to go.

The Misunderstood Goody-Two-Shoes

Life was difficult enough. But what made matters worse is that many times I felt misunderstood. It surprised me when in middle school and high school, I would get made fun of because I worked hard. I was either the nerd, the goody-two-shoes, or the overachiever. My bike was stolen after school once by one of the bullies who always called me the overachiever. There were numerous times when other students would ask why the heck I was doing homework when I had a 100 percent in the class. There seemed to be a huge misunderstanding that was creating a false perspective of who I was and what I represented.

For me it was never about the grade; it was about learning. It was never about competing against other students; it was about competing with myself. I could care less about the average class grade or what Tina made on her algebra test. My goal was to apply myself as a student.

Why were people focused on me? I wasn't focused on anyone else. Students would try to compete and wave their higher test grades in my face. I was in my own realm of curiosity, engagement, and I cared about how I spent my time. School was the only foreseeable way out of poverty, which I had to do. So to me anything less than exceptional was failing.

Maybe if some of my peers had understood my *why*, they wouldn't have called me those names. I didn't go around calling people dumb for not applying themselves. I didn't go around calling the kids with everything handed to them entitled or delusional because they lived with a security blanket. I was baffled that many failed to understand how important their current actions would affect their future. I knew it wasn't their fault; they just lacked the perspective and didn't bother trying to understand. It was sad seeing other students not care about anything, cursing out the teachers, and disrespecting the classroom.

To me it didn't make sense not to do homework. It didn't make sense to be average. It didn't make sense to cause major disruptions in the classroom. It didn't make sense to skip class. It didn't make sense not to care even though I had every reason not to care; I was poor, homeless, and surrounded by people that didn't care. According to statistics my fate was to fail; only 22 percent of homeless or impoverished students make it to college.

I may have asked a million questions in class, and I may have been the teacher's pet but I was curious to test my theory that if I used my mind, I could make my way out of poverty.

One of my peers in high school thought I was rich. Maybe it was my Ralph Lauren polo shirts my grandma helped me get. But those were from Plato's Closet and cost $5 each. I'm not really sure why he concluded that we were rich, but it goes to show that you never truly know what someone is going through until you investigate.

So before developing an opinion, do your due diligence. Before spreading negativity or false information, investigate. Growing up, some people were too quick to judge, too quick to spout an opinion. Careless comments and opinions can spread like wildfire. Just like prejudice, racism, and stereotypes can be passed down through generations. Imagine an accumulative alliance to just be better. Living your life performing acts of kindness. It starts with every mirror in the world and the people who choose to look in it.

Conclusion

Allowing yourself to view things from others' lenses helps you understand the world and people better. You become less one-sided, less narrow-minded. Your perspective will shape your values, reasoning, decisions, friendships, goals, mindset, and everything you do for the rest of your life. It's a never-ending process. That's why I invite readers to put on my shoes and walk the train tracks to get groceries and walk the busy streets of Louisville to find shelter. I invite you inside the classroom and inside the mind of an embarrassed yet determined student through the lows and highs and witness how my perspective continues to shape my opportunities. There is no right or wrong perspective, but I believe opening our minds opens more doors of opportunity.

To build perspective be an investigative journalist. Don't run with an idea without examining it. Don't form an opinion without doing your own research. Ask questions, be a skeptic, listen to others, don't condemn other people's views. Read more books, talk to more people, allow yourself to invite different views into your realm; you don't always have to agree. Step outside of the box, view the box from all six of its sides. Appreciate what you have, count your blessings, and give thanks to your supporting cast.

SUMMARY
- Make it your life-long goal to build a broader perspective.

CHAPTER 4

BUILDING A RESILIENT MINDSET

—————————————————

If you put your mind to it, you can accomplish anything.
~ Doc Brown, Back to the Future

—————————————————

I have probably seen the movie *Back to the Future* more than a hundred times in my life—once I watched it ten times in a week. The Doc Brown character, inventor of the fictional time machine, constantly repeated the above quote, and it stuck with me ever since, so much so that it became my high school senior quote. But it wasn't Doc Brown who helped me build a mindset to navigate my low points in life; that part was up to me. I needed to lay the foundational building blocks by learning how to think then applying those concepts.

Interestingly enough, there are many great books about this subject—mindset or the *growth* mindset. I'll be honest, when I was going through school, I didn't read too many books. I loved solving math problems. But after reading many of these books now as a young adult, I realize the authors were explaining everything that I had been doing to create a growth mindset, which was quite the discovery. I may not have any research, statistics, or a PhD in psychology like those authors did.

But I had the trials and tribulations of my childhood, my reflections, and my progress, so I guess you could say I have a PhD in life, and with that, I would like to share with you what I learned.

There Is a Light at the End of the Tunnel

For years during my childhood, I could never see the light at the end of the tunnel. Does that mean that it didn't exist? It depends on who you ask.

If you ask me, I never saw it between the ages of six to ten years old. But even though I didn't necessarily *see* the light, I believed it was still there. For me, it was better to believe than not, or else there was no sense of doing much of anything.

I didn't want to let my mom down. She was with me through every step and every hurdle. I couldn't afford not to believe, or else I would have been dead weight during my family's journey.

It's hard for us to understand the beauty in those difficult moments because we haven't conquered them yet. Sometimes you won't be able to reflect on it until you get through it. But I can tell you that if you believe in light at the end of the tunnel, you will be one step ahead of the rest.

Marathon Not a Sprint

When we're having a tough time not seeing the light, when we don't see progress quickly, we get worried and begin questioning everything about our capabilities. This doubt chips away at our confidence and tricks our brain to be in sprint mode. When we sprint every day, we tire ourselves out. I'm here to tell you to slow down, keep pace, and trust the process.

Trust me; I wanted progress to come quickly in my childhood, so much so that I was like a caveman, tallying the days I spent in the shelter, wondering when we would get out. Right now I want this book to be published so badly. So I understand the difficulties in wanting everything to happen *now*. But if we constantly sprint, we lose sight of the big picture and end up cutting corners.

There is a light at the end of the tunnel, and you can start seeing this light by focusing on a vision, developing awareness, and caring.

Have a Vision in Mind

Having a vision means you have some sort of idea where you want to be. A vision can be your dreams, passions, cravings, desires, or biggest wishes about being somewhere, doing something, or being something. Those dreams of receiving an award, lounging on a tropical beach, playing your favorite sport in front of millions, or being an astronaut—whether the vision is big or small—starts with visualizing the end goal.

Writing this first book, I constantly ask myself the same questions every day: *Where* is this headed? *What* does this look like at the end when everything is said and done? *Where* do I see this going in a few years? My head fills up with all of these fun ideas, and it inspires me to keep working toward those visions. So start by asking yourself the same questions. Where do *you* want to head? You may begin to discover excitement, positivity, and motivation when you start picturing that vision. But everyone has a different vision; what's yours? This type of mindset was developed during my childhood, and below were a few of my visions during those times.

When I was in the homeless shelters, I had a vision of having my own place one day.

I will never forget my first night at the homeless shelter. It was impossible to fall asleep. Without sleep I couldn't dream, and without dreams I couldn't escape the hell I was living in. But that night I kept thinking: *One of these days my family and I will get out of here. One of these days.* I had a vision of having our own house and my own room. I pictured us smiling, laughing, and being normal again. I would get excited thinking about us being back in a living room together. That was the excitement I needed to keep myself motivated. I never wanted to go back to that plastic mattress again. I didn't want to keep sharing a room with another family. I didn't want to share the same bathroom anymore. One of the most important motivations that kept me moving forward was the vision of getting out.

When I was struggling in fifth grade, I had a vision I would go to college.

I struggled to write essays. I struggled to make friends. I struggled to concentrate in class. Every day I had to hide my face because I was embarrassed by the old, short bus I had to ride because it was different from the regular school buses. I stuck out like a sore thumb. I couldn't afford haircuts. I wore the same clothes every day. But through the thick and thin of it all, I had a vision. I picked out my favorite colleges and daydreamed about walking around campus and playing baseball. I constantly told myself: *One day.* One day I would be out, and all this would be over. I didn't know how, but I knew because that vision was real. Envision yourself where you want to be.

When I was in middle school, I had a vision that I would be on television.

I loved acting in middle school, whether I performed monologues or auditioned for the lead role in the school plays, I just loved the concept of becoming a new character. It was such a fun outlet. I think I enjoyed it so much because I got to escape the person I was embarrassed of being. I also loved to entertain people and make them laugh; it was always in my nature. It was also like medicine to me. I had a vision that one day I would be on a big screen or on television.

When I was in high school, I had a vision that I was going to be valedictorian.

When I was in eighth grade my brother told me I could be valedictorian. He said it would help me get to college, and I would be able to speak at graduation. I didn't even know what that word meant at the time, but it sounded intriguing.

He said, "The only tough part is you need all As every semester, so you can't mess up your freshman year—no pressure."

On that day the challenge started, and the vision became real.

When I was in college, I had a vision of being at the top of the class, as an engineer, holding my college degree.

At orientation, they gathered all the pre-engineering students in a room and told us something along the lines of: *Look around you right now. Half of you will fail or change majors by the end of the first semester and the other half will have a GPA below 3.0.*

I thought: *What a great way to motivate students.* It made me nervous, but it inspired the vision of proving them wrong. I didn't want to be a part of another statistic; I'd come too far along to fall short.

What do all of these visions have in common? They all came true in some sort of fashion. Some people call it luck. While I'm sure half of it is luck, the other half was staying true to myself with the vision always in mind. When you have a vision, you have a direction. Let your visions be guided by your dreams, passions, and biggest wishes.

Develop a Sense of Awareness

To get one step closer to your vision, you need to develop a better sense of awareness, which is all about forming perception of both ourselves and our environment. Developing a positive sense of awareness is one of the hardest and longest steps through our tunnel because sometimes our environment, or outside forces, cannot be controlled. Our environment—whether people's words, our living situation, or a lack of resources—can have a high probability of crashing the tunnel we were navigating through. And awareness can differ between ages, too. An eight-year-old's mind thinks differently than someone in college. The priorities of those two groups are vastly different. But is there such a thing as too young to begin to develop a sense of awareness? I don't think so.

Awareness of attitude

As a six-year-old, I couldn't control that cancer stole my mother away. As an impoverished seven-year-old, I couldn't control that my family was evicted from our house. As a homeless eight-year-old, I couldn't control that I was living in a shelter, sharing a bunk bed with my family. As a fortunate twelve-year-old, I couldn't control that we were living in a tiny house with no Internet access and a lack of transportation. As an eighteen-year-old, I couldn't control that I was homeless yet again right before graduation and college.

But what I could control was my attitude regarding these situations. Sure, I may have whined a little because it was tough. But ultimately I chose to take a glass-half-full attitude. Things could always be worse. I was fortunate to be living in a shelter versus living on the streets. I was fortunate to be with my family rather than being alone. I was fortunate to still be able to play sports. I was fortunate to have a roof over my head. I was fortunate to have a college acceptance and scholarship. The more I realized that things could always be worse was when my awareness of my attitude began to take shape. Who was I to complain?

Once I captured that idea, I tried to make more positive days than most. It became a balance and a challenge I enjoyed. There was a consistent puzzle around me that needed to be solved, which is probably why I became an engineer.

Some problems appear daunting, and there's a lot of noise around them, but picking them apart and struggling through them ultimately becomes your building blocks of growth. It all starts with the attitude toward your problems.

Let's say if I consistently drank from the glass-half-empty attitude, what would that have accomplished long term? Would I have continued the cycle of poverty with my own family? Would I have never cared all the way up to high school? When we have a glass-half-empty attitude, we tend to not care about particular things in our life, including our attitude, presence, school, friends, or much of anything.

When we don't care about things, there are never incentives or motivations to do anything. When we choose to see the glass-half-empty we believe there is no light at the end of the tunnel. If I never cared up until high school, then I would have never become valedictorian. I might have dropped out of high school, which would have put me in an even deeper, darker tunnel than I was before.

Instead I'm alive and well, typing my heart out to show the light to anyone who needs to believe, to show that you can do anything and everything you put your mind to.

Awareness of our days

Your attitude and outlook immediately affect your motivation to do anything. Being aware of your attitude toward and outlook about your situation can help you become mindful of how you spend your days, which in turn enables you to reflect on how you can improve them. How will you know what to improve if you don't know how you spent them? If you ask yourself the following questions and can answer them, you will be one step ahead:

>What did you do yesterday that you could do better today?
>
>What are some things you could do today to accomplish your vision?
>
>Are you aware of what your priorities are for what you need to be doing?

When I was in school, I had the vision of making it to college, regardless of what was in front of me: the tuition costs, poverty, or any other outside forces. The vision was present, but what about the awareness? What did I do yesterday that I could do better today? I observed the world around me and made mental notes of what worked and what didn't. I observed that not studying, skipping class, wasting time, and not taking notes didn't contribute anything positive toward my vision, so why would I waste my time that way?

Even to this day, I try to develop a sense of awareness about my days. Whether it's reflecting at the end of the day or journaling about what worked and what didn't. Some days I was lazy, other days I knocked out pages of work. Developing a sense of awareness will be an ongoing battle throughout your life. There is no getting around it or taking any shortcuts. But the choice to continue and the choice to start developing that sense of awareness is up to you.

Being aware keeps you more in tune with the world around you. Sometimes we get so caught up in everything else in our environment that we don't take time to reflect on what we're doing for ourselves. I think it's great to be selfish sometimes; it's a good way to always make sure that you're doing what you need to for your own well-being.

The Art of Caring

Aside from developing a vision and awareness, there is one thing you can't necessarily teach: how to care. That will only develop when you choose to.

Sometimes it's tough to identify what we love and care about when we feel as if the world doesn't care about us. Sometimes our family and friends abandon us. Sometimes we get denied, and sometimes we don't feel accepted, as if the world is completely against us. Sometimes not caring is cool because we like to be different; we like to be rebels because that is what is delivering us the most attention. Sometimes we just need attention, acceptance, love, and acknowledgment but just aren't getting enough. What is there to love and care about if we are constantly rejected by the people we love and care about the most?

Like I mentioned before, you can't teach someone how to care. But if you choose to live, there has to be something you can identify. You're still waking up in the mornings, you haven't ended it yet. If you can't identify something you care about, then identify reasons why you don't care. Why do you not care about learning? Why do you not care about your family? Why do you not care about doing better? And *just because* isn't an answer.

This is called the merry-go-round of solving our own problems. For the physics nerds, we know that when a merry-go-round spins, the largest force is on the outer edge. The more we stay on the outer edge, avoiding the middle, the more difficult it is to turn the ride off. There's a huge off button in the middle, and many obstacles along the way, including carriages, horses, lions—you name it. The more we avoid our problems, the longer we'll be on the outer edge and sooner or later we'll *fall off*.

I don't want anyone to fall off. I want you to cry for help and be willing to force your way to the middle of the ride.

Never forget about your visions, ideals, dreams, and passions. Even if the world poses its negative influences on us, we still have ourselves to take care of. We'll be taking care of ourselves for many years to come. So with that in mind, stay true to yourself and your ideals when outside forces seem to be closing in. Identify what you know to be true about yourself and understand you have the potential to be better.

Caring is what you cry about at night. Caring is that feeling you get in your stomach full of butterflies. Caring is that feeling of want and desire. It's what makes you tick, and it's what you think about constantly. It's deep down in there, you just have to find it. If you don't care about anything, you're not going to do anything about it. If you don't care about your homework, you're probably not going to get it done. If you don't care about your friends, you're probably not going to spend time with them.

Are you aware of what you love the most? Do you care about the things that you're doing right now? Once you figure out what you care about and what you love, it will give you something to look forward to in your mornings.

You're the Captain of Your Ship, the Director of Your Movie, and the Author of Your Story

Having a vision, building awareness, and identifying what you care about are great steps toward seeing the light at the end of the long, dark, tunnel. There are also other ways to keep you on track to build a resilient mindset.

Understanding that you're the captain of your own ship, the director of your movie, and the author of your own book is a very motivating outlook to have that could change your life. There can be many strong winds and other creatures you meet along the way at sea, but you're the captain of your own decisions. The more aware you are of your vision, the more you know the course you're sailing.

Each and every action you make is the story you're writing. Do you want a happy ending or a sad ending? Will you write something you'll be proud of?

You're the director and star of your own movie. Who do you want in the cast? Hopefully you assemble a strong supporting cast, including your friends, mentors, family, and coworkers. Your supporting cast matters because those are the people helping tell your story throughout the entire movie. As a director, you can have multiple casting calls until you find the right ones. At times we feel forced into negative friendships or relationships that appear impossible to break away from. Develop the awareness of how that could be altered or changed.

Most importantly, you're the star. And a star radiates light. The more you accept your role as the star and the more you work to develop your role, the larger the light in your deep, dark tunnel.

Why Do We Give Up?

I gave up sometimes because of fear, low self-esteem, and impatience.
Fear
There was a never-ending cycle of fears that created a roadblock between where I needed to go and where I was scared to go.

What if people see where I live?

What if people find out I'm poor?

What if they see me walking home from a grocery trip?
What do I say when they ask why?
There was also a fear of failing and fear of the unknown.
Where was my next meal coming from?

What happens if I fail out of school?
Why did I feel that lump in my throat, and why did my heart used to skip beats? Why did my stomach fill up with painful butterflies? Regardless of how I was feeling, it wasn't going to disappear if I didn't do anything about it. Luckily, the quote *never give up* was there to remind me every day. I began to separate the things I could control from the things I couldn't.

I couldn't control other people's opinions or questions. I couldn't control living in a shelter. I couldn't control the fact that my feet were one of my only forms of transportation. What I could control was my attitude. I could control my goals, my approach, and my actions. Every day posed another fear, or opportunity, and it was up to me to decide if I was going to give up or step up to the plate.

Low self-esteem

Throughout my time living in a homeless shelter, I often thought: *Does any of this matter anyway? I'm never going to make it out of here.* Life wasn't perfect, and I wasn't always Mr. Positive. There were days where I was unmotivated, which burned my self-esteem. At times it was so bad that I didn't even want to show my face.

Just like life, I struck out many times during baseball too. That didn't mean I didn't know how to play. What made the difference is I always stepped up to the plate. You might even have the fans sitting on the bleachers try to derail your value. But leave the noise on the bleachers and get ready in the batter's box. They weren't there with you when you were in the batting cage all day the day before.

Lack of patience

It's hard not to get impatient when we crave it now. And when progress doesn't show, we get worried, and then we start to question if we will ever obtain what we've always wanted.

This sounds like a slump. Any great baseball player has had one. A slump is when, for a period of time, you can't hit the ball even if your life depended on it. It's like you completely forgot how to even swing a baseball bat.

Trust the process, and trust all your efforts and hard work in the batting cage. Be patient in the batter's box. The base hit will come. And soon, with a strong enough mindset, you can start hitting home runs.

Stay on "Track"

My dad and I walked the train tracks every time we needed to get groceries. The train tracks brought us closer as we talked about life, the future, mom, and baseball.

A little bit of love can go a long way. It was through my love for my dad and my admiration of his fight that I was able to build my own perseverance. The train track walks taught me that not everyone in this world gets handed things; sometimes we actually have to go out and get them.

When you're trying to survive, you have to do anything and everything or else things become infinitely worse. Think of what you would like to accomplish and imagine that you had everything to lose. Use this concept throughout your work to stay on track.

SUMMARY

In order to build a resilient mindset:
- Believe there is a light at the end of the tunnel.
- Develop a vision of your goals, aspirations, and the ending to the story you're writing.
- Develop a sense of awareness around your attitude and your days.
- Identify what you love and care about the most.
- Be the captain of your ship, the director of your movie, and the author of your story.

CHAPTER 5

USE YOUR
TIME WISELY

How you spend your days is how you spend your life.
~ Annie Dillard

In middle school I sprinted so hard to the next class that I burned the insoles of my shoes; no wonder why I have feet problems today. Every second wasted was a second taken away from me finishing my homework. I calculated it out: I had five minutes between bells, so this meant if I got to class in under a minute I could utilize those remaining four minutes for finishing homework. Multiplying those four minutes by the number of bells in the day gave me twenty minutes to do something.

I did this because it was my goal to never have homework—ever. The second reason was I discovered that time was finite. Like gold, we can't just make more out of thin air. The clock is continually ticking, and the present becomes the past after each tick. So at the young age of nine, I began asking myself: *Why would I waste this precious resource?*

This method seems extreme, and you're right, I should have given my poor feet a break. But it made all of the difference. If there was anything I learned, it was how to use my time wisely, and I would like to share a couple of key principles I learned along the way.

Make an Effort, Not an Excuse

We can blame everything and everyone around us, but eventually there comes a time when we have to look in the mirror. Excuses are our biggest roadblocks. Excuses will always be there for you, opportunity won't. Below are two of the common excuses I heard growing up and what I hear today.

I don't have time.

> Tomorrow (noun): A mystical land where 90 percent of all human productivity, motivation, and achievement is stored.

It appears no one has time to do anything. We have this place called tomorrow to use as an excuse. But one thing is for certain: tomorrow isn't promised.

We somehow have time to scroll through Facebook, watch all of our friend's Snapchat stories, post a two-paragraph status update, casually walk around the mall, spend hours creating a TikTok dance video, and watch television. But we can't find time for our priorities; those tend to get shoved to the side.

I don't know enough about it.

I think this translates more to: *I don't care enough about it.* Because if you truly are interested in something, you have a higher probability of learning about it. Have you ever been curious about something then you immediately Googled it? That's essentially what it takes for you to figure out where to start. Sometimes it's as simple as getting out your phone and Googling or watching a YouTube video.

I could have made many excuses for not completing my assignments, but I chose not to. I didn't have a computer or Internet to complete many assignments. I could have made the excuse that I didn't know enough about the subject. I could have blamed my living situation. So why were others making excuses? Beats me. If there comes a time when you're facing an excuse, just be honest with yourself and always remember: *Make an effort, not an excuse.*

Those Daunting Priorities, the Destruction of Escapism

According to the *Cambridge English Dictionary*, *escapism* is "a way of avoiding an unpleasant or boring life, especially by thinking, reading, etc., about more exciting but impossible activities."

Escapism is a mental diversion often used to distract yourself from persistent feelings of depression or general sadness. Growing up, I saw many students hop into the realm of escapism, and some of us are caught doing it today outside of school. Priorities and escapism seem to have a linear relationship; when priorities stack up, so does the time spent escaping them.

Our parents and teachers tell us to do our homework, study for our tests, and make good grades. The weight of the world feels like it's on our shoulders. Sometimes we push our priorities away because the due date isn't near. We hop on our phones or play video games to escape our current reality. We scroll, scroll, scroll, click, click, click.

Do you know what your current screen time is for the day?

More importantly, was it mindless scrolling or productive?

Leisure is important but so are priorities; there's a never-ending balancing act. It doesn't have to be a hard sprint to be 100 percent perfect with accomplishing priorities. But if this balance is consistently leaning more toward leisure, and not toward priorities related to your goals, then let's take a step back and discover the value of time.

The Value of Time

You need to discover the value of time to use it wisely. The choice to make this discovery will be up to you. I can only explain to you how valuable it is.

I discovered the value of time in sixth grade after I moved to Florida from Kentucky, which I consider to be the restart of my life. My family was finally able to leave behind the trials and tribulations of our hometown. We faced a new journey ahead. School and sports were all I had to make it out of poverty.

The discovery came from the same story in the beginning of this chapter—the one where I darted through the halls to get to class. Each day became a new opportunity to be more productive. It was always a challenge to see how much work I could get done. I wondered if I could get to the point of never having homework. The teachers would display the classwork, homework problems, and the respective textbook pages on the white board, so why not? I'd open up the textbook and knock out everything I could before the class began.

Why would I sit there and waste time doing nothing? There was nothing productive about that mindset. Even five to ten minutes could foster learning or an accomplishment. The question was how to measure time's value in the first place. The answer came from seeing the results. I remember my first progress report week like it was yesterday, and I still have the progress report for proof.

One class after another, I handed mine over to the teacher to be marked for a grade. The first grade came back as an A, which felt awesome. Then there was another A and then another, until finally at the end of the day there were all As. I had never felt so accomplished. There was no better measurement of the value of time than witnessing that my input was producing great output that felt good, felt right. I knew I was doing what I was supposed to be doing. There was a lot of positive reinforcement coming from my teachers, family, and myself. Most importantly, I was fostering a deep learning of the material. The grades I made always made sense because I understood the material.

Now, the opposite of using time is rolling into class late, never pulling a notebook out, and going in with the attitude of doing the minimum to get through. Doing the absolute minimum minimizes your potential.

It's never too late to discover the value of time, but the clock is ticking.

Continue loving the value of time

You might have discovered the value of time, and you might have gotten super motivated one or two days and accomplished a lot. But that's just one or two days out of your entire life. What about the other 25,000 days you're going to spend? Those mere couple of inspirational days are roughly 0.005 percent of the rest of your life. We can never forget to lose sight of the value of time.

I continued loving the value of time through the rest of middle school, high school, college, and even today in my career. I fell in love with a few questions—*How could I be better today? What can I do right now to make that happen?*—and with the process of answering those questions. What's magical about this is I'm not even in school anymore. These questions can stay with you forever if you let them.

Every single day I get out a notebook, computer, or phone, and I write. It doesn't even matter what I write as long as I'm writing. I could be writing lyrics, my game plan for the day, journal entries, or diagrams of engineering concepts. These are a few things that jump start my day. The most important thing is that I use my time doing things I love. I was fortunate to wake up and see another day, and that's the most I could ever ask for. I plan to get the most out of each and every day.

And on days when I'm feeling tired or bogged down, I listen to my body. Resting is using your time wisely too, never forget that.

What are you doing with the time you have? What areas in your life are you willing to sacrifice to create more time? Is there anything you're trying to accomplish? What's holding you back? If time is the answer, have you done enough to try and create that time? If you haven't tried as hard as you can—as if your life, all your goals, and your family depended on it—then you might not have tried hard enough. Being honest with yourself is the first step. The next step is action.

Those extra hours make a difference

Sometimes you can't always use your smarts to figure things out. Sometimes you need to rely on your stamina. Sometimes it takes late nights and extra hours. Those times when you're pushed to the edge of defeat but you push back harder for one extra hour are the special moments when our brains stretch and grow. Despite the pressure, you hold strong because you care and accept the sacrifice. It takes a special person to keep pushing forward. And you are a special person deep inside, whether you believe it or not. You just have to tap into it. No one else can see the work you do behind closed doors. At least no one saw it through my lens, and it made all the difference.

In college, my Calculus II class was unreasonably difficult, and I broke my first rule: I made an excuse and blamed the professor. The professor was too quick, the tests were long, and the time was short. But in order to accomplish my goal, I had to rely on effort, not an excuse.

So I managed my Calculus II class by using my time wisely and working hard. This was my freshman year of college and there were invitations to parties and events left and right. I lived in Tallahassee, a college town where access to fun was a step away. The peer pressure was strong and the guilt became real when I often avoided going out. It was difficult because I wanted to avoid being the lame kid that studied all the time, so I had to balance my efforts. There was an understanding early on that my main priorities in college were to grow and graduate, not party my way to failure. I didn't have a safety net if I dropped out. But don't get me wrong, I had loads of fun—boy, I have some stories.

Balancing work and play was not easy by any means. Hard work never is; that's why it's called hard work. Sometimes we will need to do things we don't necessarily feel like doing. There are no secrets; it just comes down to true dedication, commitment, and discipline.

If you want it badly enough, you can achieve it. I wanted it so badly that I spent multiple days doing practice problems in the book until I knew how to do each one. I isolated myself in my room for hours on end and eliminated all distractions. I watched countless Youtube videos. I wanted it so badly that I missed out on my favorite musician's concert. It sounds extreme, but no one could take away the hard work I put in, and the results were the testament. And I don't regret how I spent my time because it was *exactly* what I wanted and needed to do. Those extra hours sure made a difference and they can for you too.

Using time wisely

When you go through school, not only will you need to learn the material, but you'll need to learn how to study to best learn. Studying can take a large portion of your time, especially if you don't use your time wisely. Below are some of my key study tips that helped me stay on track.

Eliminate all distractions, which include your phone, social media tabs on your browser, friends, and noise. Those micro-minutes of checking your phone, scrolling through TikTok, or talking to your friends add up. There was a reason why I refused to study in groups and avoided crowded libraries. Next time you need to study, politely refuse your friends, and turn off your phone. When you cut the distractions, you'll soon realize how much time you can create for yourself.

Develop a consistent routine. Whether you blare your favorite artist on the loudspeakers, eat mints every thirty minutes, or whatever the case may be, try to develop a consistent routine before studying. Now, this doesn't mean doing the same exact thing every day; that would be mundane. What I mean is narrow down a process that works for you. In college I figured out what worked and what didn't work. I learned that I studied better at night and determined that I hated sitting on the couch or in bed when I studied. Finding your best routine will help create more time for yourself in the long term.

Reward yourself. Before you begin studying, establish a reward system. Not only will this give you incentive to complete the task, but you will feel a sense of accomplishment if you finish what you were supposed to. In college I really enjoyed ice cream as my reward. My ice cream was my light at the end of the tunnel. When you provide a reward, you'll focus more on completing the task at hand, and you'll end up saving more time in the long run.

Don't copy answers from the back of the book. We've all done this. I'm not perfect. But doing it didn't push me in a positive direction in college, so I had to make a change. Instead, I would treat the problem as if it were a test. I would write out everything I knew about the question and what I needed to know to answer the question. If I were truly stuck, I would research the first step, typically on Chegg or in the textbook. Instead of reviewing the entire process, I would leave myself breadcrumbs if I ran through roadblocks. Then after I finished the problem, I'd try again, and again, and again until I could do each problem on my own. And not only that, but I would also make sure I picked out problems that had slight variations because anything can happen on a test. You need to be ready for the curveballs the professor throws at you. This approach is using time wisely because cheating—or being lazy—is a waste of time and isn't worth it in the long run as you already learned in the previous chapter.

Take Notes

I'm twenty-five years old, three years out of school, and I still take notes. I draw on the whiteboard at work, I take notes in meetings, I jot down concepts, I draw pictures, I write out a game plan each night for the next day, I write in a journal about my daily events, I share my ideas, and write raps in the Notes app on my iPhone. Of the 379 notes, most likely 75 percent of those are rap lyrics, which are about enough to make a few mixtapes. I have archived the notes I took in my college physics, calculus, structural analysis, and steel design courses. I list and analyze my investments and have written out my retirement plan.

I take a lot of notes. Always have and I never plan to stop. It's a very useful habit. I started early, sometime in kindergarten. And ever since then my mind discovered another world. It allows me to reflect, to gain clarity, to remember, to learn, to stay on track—the list goes on.

In fact, note-taking is backed by research. Studies published in the journal *Educational Psychologist* have shown that students who reviewed notes showed superior performance on measures of learning than students who did not review notes. Students also gain advantage with long-term memory and taking notes has a direct relationship to how much information students retain. Based on these studies alone, I would highly suggest writing more information down from lectures and taking the time to review it later. The only difficult part of taking notes is making the effort.

As a ten-year-old kid, I didn't need scientific studies to understand that notes were beneficial. The only statistics I needed to see were the As on my report card. Whether I was jotting down everything the teacher was saying or writing on my own time, notes helped me process and retain information at a faster pace.

Note-taking goes beyond the classroom. When I got my internship at the civil engineering company as a college sophomore, I had never read construction plans before. I hadn't even stepped foot in an engineering class yet. The first week of the internship the team called a meeting in the small, fishbowl of a conference room. I rushed to the meeting, eager to hear the ins and outs of the work planned for the week.

I stepped in the fishbowl and immediately received a couple of confused stares.

My supervisor asked, "You got anything to write with? Go get a pen and paper."

It was a reminder that even in the real world, we should consider taking notes.

Plan Your Days

Like my brother always says: *If you fail to plan you plan to fail.* NFL coaches develop game plans throughout the week to build an edge against their opponent. Teachers game plan their lessons to make sure their students learn. Project managers develop game plans months in advance to maintain their projects' efficiency. The same concept can be applied to our lives; developing a plan keeps you on track. With a game plan you have direction. And with direction you create your own sense of accountability, especially if you write the game plan down and make it real.

Before I go to sleep, I develop a game plan for the next day. I keep a journal of my ideas, goals, thoughts, and feelings. When I don't accomplish what's on my game plan, I feel bad about it. But that means that I cared enough about it to let it affect me. Feeling bad is good in this case because it makes me want to do better the next day.

Keep in mind that there are beauties to both sides of completing the game plan and not. If you didn't complete anything on your game plan, hopefully you can at least ask yourself why you didn't. The answers can vary widely, but as long as you're aware of what happened, you can identify how to improve. This process transcends beyond the classroom and continues throughout your life. So what will you game plan today?

SUMMARY
- How you spend your days is how you spend your life.
- Make an effort, not an excuse.
- Avoid escapism and take action.
- Eliminate distractions.
- Game plan your days.

CHAPTER 6

YOU'RE GOING TO
FAIL YOUR ENTIRE LIFE

Failure is not the opposite of success; it's part of success.
~ Arianna Huffington

Even the valedictorians and those who graduate magna cum laude fail from time to time, take it from me. Here is my long list:

I failed my multiplication table test five times in third grade

I failed my first essay in fifth grade

I failed multiple AP exams

I failed at obtaining my target score for the SAT

I failed my first assignment in college

I failed my first two internships and didn't land the job

I failed many of my first tasks as a new hire at my first job

Glancing at this list, it's easy to say that this guy is a complete failure. A straight-A student is not supposed to fail. Valedictorians pass all of their classes and tests, right? Everything comes natural for the nerds of the class.

I am here to say first-hand that is far from true.

Among some of my peers being gifted was a stigma because from their perspective everything came natural for me. The truth was I failed many times and nothing came easy. The other students only saw the times when I made good grades. What separated me from others was my response to failure. It took years to understand that failure was inevitable. No matter what we do throughout our lives, there will come a time when we fail. The real question is what are we going to do about it?

Failing the Multiplication Table Test

When you fail you should feel bad; that means you care enough about it. But this emotional response can end up being positive or negative, depending on your choice.

In third grade I failed my multiplication test five different times. The first time I failed the test, I didn't do anything about it. I felt bad and felt like a failure, but I still chose not to study hard the next time. The second time I failed, I began to think that math wasn't my strong suit and that I would magically pass the next time because of my experience with the first test. I failed again. To make matters worse, I was one of the final three students that hadn't passed the test, and the teacher made it known to the classroom, so boy was I embarrassed.

After I failed my fourth time, I finally said enough is enough! I wasn't going to be the only kid left. I didn't want to repeat third grade. I finally made the decision to examine my previous tests and asked the questions: *What went wrong? What are my weaknesses? What are my strengths?*

I reflected deeply about how in the world I could pass the test. And yes I was only eight years old reflecting on my life. I took my copies back to the homeless shelter and starred all the easy ones that I knew how to do. Then I circled the ones that gave me mild trouble. I didn't spend much time on those.

Last but not least it was the daunting ones—the pesky sixes and eights—that always seemed to confuse me. I spent many nights awake, drawing pictures, memorizing, timing myself, doing whatever I could to pass the test. I think you can probably guess the ending of the story: I passed the test, and I actually beat the record time of the entire class—taking the test five times no doubt helped.

If you take away anything from this story, remember that you have the choice about which direction you want failure to lead you. It will always be your response to failure that will ultimately define you. It is too easy to let our failures dictate our value. You have the potential to accomplish anything you want to, as long as you put your mind to it. Use failure as a guide of how to do better next time.

Ironically, math became my favorite subject in school, which led me to love calculus, physics, and engineering. Math could have derailed my entire academic career and even my professional career today had I let it affect my sense of value. It would've been way too easy to call myself a failure and say that I was just bad at math. It's really easy to tell yourself that you're just not good at something. I always told people in school that they could be good at math as long as they put the time in. I was just like everyone else. I was in the bottom of the bunch and worked hard every year to get better and better at math.

The next time you fail, ask yourself: what could I do better next time?

It's never too early to start building the foundation for a better future. It sounds crazy, but failing is going to be the best thing that you ever do but only if you use your failures wisely. I know from experience it is difficult to understand the rewards of failure as you're going through it. But now it's easy for me to look back and reflect from my current perspective, which should be motivation for you.

True failure isn't failing a test or failing an assignment. It's allowing an event to defeat you and hold you back from accomplishing your goals.

The next time you feel down or you feel like you failed, take a step back and ask: *What direction will I choose to go?*

SUMMARY
- Failure is inevitable; your choice to do better next time isn't.
- Use your emotional response to failure wisely.
- True failure is letting something you failed at defeat you.

CHAPTER 7

STAY CURIOUS

If knowledge is power, then curiosity is the muscle.
~ Danielle LaPorte

Curiosity may have killed the cat, but in people it sparks conversation, questions, and the good kind of revolutions that we need in our lives to advance not only as individuals but as groups of people.

If Nikola Tesla had never been curious about electricity, then we would be centuries behind in our advancement as a civilization. Now, I know some of us aren't meant to create the next life-changing invention of the century, and some of us are probably barely scraping by in algebra, but with enough curiosity we can change our lives for the better. This chapter will examine the many long-term benefits of maintaining curiosity in your daily life.

How to Become Curious

Everyone has different interests. So it may be difficult to actually zone in on certain topics that don't appeal to our interests. And curiosity should feel natural, not forced. Based on my experience, I believe curiosity begins with observing the world around you, generating an interest, asking a question, and taking action on answering the question.

Let's dive into an example of how curiosity is created and developed. In sixth grade I observed each subject. Low and behold, I gained an interest in math, due to the idea that there was a problem to be solved. And this feeling I had didn't feel forced; it came from within due to my desire to learn and better myself.

I then asked the question: *What can I do right now to better understand?* The question was then followed up by an action: I opened up the textbook and began to read ahead into the next chapter. Each day I asked a new question, which gave me direction to try and answer. The important lesson here is to start by examining the world around you, generate an interest, ask a question, and take action.

I always found myself wanting to know more. I viewed every topic as a never-ending strand of opportunity. Each strand had other intertwining loops that opened up new doors for learning. Asking *how* and *why* became a life-changing habit that would ultimately transform the way I moved through time.

In college when I realized calculus and physics had interrelated strands, I began noticing more patterns, which became more and more intriguing. I would read ahead in both textbooks to relate the two topics together. The extra time spent reading allowed me to formulate questions for class. Getting the right questions answered and recognizing patterns made the nasty alien calligraphy of physics equations easier to comprehend and ultimately made my future classes easier.

Not everyone is an engineer or rocket scientist, so how does this apply to non-STEM majors? Curiosity can be applied to anyone. English majors have to write long essays and research papers. The first thing an English major could ask themselves is: *How can I efficiently write this paper?* That seems like a good start. Questioning how can help generate ideas on how to better manage time, outline, and organization.

The next question may be: *How can I invoke a stronger feeling in this paragraph?* That question can lead to learning more synonyms, sentence structure, and may even spark an interest in studying other authors and their writing styles.

You can pick any type of major or career path and it holds true. An actor could ask: *How can I capture the crowd in this scene?* An accountant could ask: *How can I develop a better means of monitoring my business's revenue?* If you never wonder how, you'll never try to understand.

Curiosity can spark an infinite appetite of hunger that can ultimately lead to feasts of learning. The more curious you are, the more your brain muscle can flex. And the more your brain muscle can flex, the better your brain can process and connect dots in the future.

Be a Sponge with Information

You'll ultimately be a sponge of information if you're a sponge *with* information. Try absorbing anything and everything you can—without hurting yourself. During your school career, you will have information bouncing toward you left and right. It will be your job to capture and store it for your use. School is one big test on how well you can retain information.

The best means of retaining information is relentless absorption and repetition. Keep in mind, absorption is not possible without a willingness to absorb. With anything and everything you do, you'll need to build the discipline to want to do it. That is the ultimate test. Once you get over that hump, the rest falls in place. Strive to be a sponge, be inevitably porous with learning. Absorption is the only way of life for a sponge, as it can be for you.

During the first month of my career I dedicated a large amount of time to being a sponge. In a matter of a few months, I helped transform our office's file structure, design process, and design templates. I was curious about how we could be more efficient. I absorbed as much as I could about our current design procedures and files, our team's input, researching engineering textbooks, and learning new design software.

Although I spent hours after work and sacrificed weekends, I genuinely enjoyed the journey to help build our foundation. The bigger picture was always about being better. It was easy to view learning as a hobby instead of a job. I understand people can't always stay late because they have kids or other priorities—however, I can't stress enough that staying curious isn't dependent on staying late or putting in large amounts of time, which leads me to the next important theme.

Learning Something New Can Take Minutes

Even ten minutes out of your day can open up an endless number of opportunities. The Internet is a powerful tool that is readily available at your fingertips, so make use of it!

Speaking of the Internet, I'm sure we all can relate to finding ourselves meaninglessly scrolling our minutes away. Soon enough it's either time for bed or time to complete our next priority, only to find that our phone battery— and mental battery— are drained. What if we took those minutes of unproductive scrolling and converted them into productive minutes? Instead of scrolling through Becky's Instagram page, maybe we can head to Twitter or YouTube and follow someone worthwhile who is working toward goals similar to ours.

Over the years, I have built YouTube playlists where I store videos related to my interests. Every day I find myself looking up a video to learn something new. Try creating your own playlists of things you love. Consider taking a few minutes each day to watch a video and store it on a playlist. I have also learned a lot on Twitter because I follow certain people and profiles that are more in line with my goals. It has completely opened up a new door for learning, networking, and helping me reach my goals versus scrolling my life away.

The complete power is held in our hands—literally.

Be Curious with How You Spend Your Days

One day I woke up extremely curious. I got out a fresh, white piece of paper and a pen and began writing an entire plan for my morning routine. I was curious how long each of these steps actually took and if I could increase my efficiency. The plan made me focus on each goal set forth on the piece of paper. I wrote out all the important activities I wanted to complete. It looked something like this:

Morning Routine:

5:00 a.m. – 5:10 a.m.: Wake up and be out of bed, don't snooze alarm

5:10 a.m. – 5:20 a.m.: Start breakfast, throw clothes in dryer

5:20 a.m. – 5:40 a.m.: Finish breakfast, read news, read chapter of book

5:40 a.m. – 6:40 a.m.: Write a chapter

With each activity I would write an update on how long it actually took to complete, so I knew how to reconstruct my plan next time. It was fun to see each activity as a challenge and try to complete it as fast as I could, especially if it were breakfast or chores, which were essential but were taking time away from writing and studying. The more time I could create for myself, the better.

Once I narrowed down how long each activity took, my morning routine became more like a dance rehearsal. The apartment was my center stage, and I was the lead actor. I often imagined a director filming the documentary that was my life. I would skip to the coffee machine, shuffle the clothes in the washer, flip the microwave door open with elegance. Each accomplished task provided an extra boost of energy that carried me through the heart of the day.

The first time I ever made the morning game plan, I ended up with forty-five extra minutes at my disposal! It was so eye-opening to me that I had accomplished a lot of these mundane tasks in no time at all. To some people that might be a bit much, and you probably think that Griffin is on his happy drugs or something, which is rightfully so. But the outcome was worth way more than other people's opinions. I developed something that changed my daily outlook and life forever. All because I woke up feeling curious.

If you spend your days searching instead of despairing, life becomes more of an investigation, which can result in a monumental discovery. You have the choice to be an investigative journalist. If you're curious about anything, inspect it. Then remember the process: observe, develop an interest, ask a question, then take action. The answers are out there, so stay curious and learn something new each day.

SUMMARY
- Curiosity is an infinite appetite of hunger that gets fulfilled with feasts of learning.
- Be a sponge with information.
- Begin asking how and why more often throughout your days.
- Learning something new can take five minutes.
- Never stop being curious.

CHAPTER 8

IT'S OKAY TO ASK FOR HELP

Asking for help isn't a sign of weakness, it's a sign of strength. It shows you have the courage to admit when you don't know something, and to learn something new.
~ Barack Obama

The thing I was most embarrassed about growing up was asking for help. Throughout my school career, this embarrassment made me sick, but it was often unavoidable. I never had enough cash to go on dates, I always needed rides to school, and I always had to go out of my way to use someone's computer to complete my assignments. Whenever I would ask for help, there were typically follow-up questions that I often tried to dodge, like: *Why don't you have a car?* or *What does your family do?* I dodged all the questions because I didn't want to be the poor kid. And I didn't want anyone's pity either. I just wanted people to accept me for who I was, not where I came from or what I was going through.

It was never fun being in the homeless shelter waiting for a ride to my baseball game. It was never fun asking for a ride home from the grocery store. It was never fun asking to use someone's computer. But in order to move forward and conquer my fear, I couldn't let the disease of embarrassment become a terminal case. One thing that often helped me persevere was thinking ahead toward my future. This chapter explores some of the few challenges and hurdles it took to overcome such fear and showcases why you should never be afraid to ask for help.

Why We're Afraid to Ask Questions

"I don't want to always rely on others."

It's tough when you have to ask your peers to use their Internet, computer, and get rides to school. It's tough to ask random people for money in order to eat and get a hotel for the night. I've been there before, and I will say this: you can do anything you put your mind to, but sometimes you have to bite the bullet and ask. Each and every one of us is a product of helping hands, and this will never change through life. To keep climbing the ladder to growth, we will need help from others.

Like the old saying goes: It takes a village.

"I have too many questions."

I's awesome that you have a million questions; that means you're thinking! However, if you think this is holding you back, identify the critical path questions, which are those that need an answer to move forward with the assignment. If you're ever handed an assignment, task, or mission, try to complete everything you know how to do. That way you're still using time wisely. If you think you have a million questions, document them and save them for when the time is right.

"I don't want to bother anyone."

Everyone is busy and everyone is up to something, our teachers, friends, peers. It's difficult to conquer this fear. To get over this hurdle, try to view it from the opposite perspective. Imagine you're the one being asked for help. It's almost an honor to be asked for help because someone sees us as a reliable source.

Now, it never helps when we're trying to ask someone a question and they appear flustered or bothered. This type of energy makes it difficult because we feel like we can't approach them. Sometimes it can be the other person, although half the time it can be our own insecurity. But let me tell you, if it's your job to get a task done, you won't be bothering anyone. Think of it as you're doing exactly what you need to be doing. Think of it as if you didn't ask, you're not doing the job. So do your job! Act like your work depends on it.

"I don't want to sound dumb."

This is the most common fear holding us back from asking questions. We're afraid of stumbling, we're afraid of our voice, our word choice, and of asking something that will come across as ill-informed or ignorant. All eyes and ears are aimed at us and the last thing we want to do is mess up. It's easy for others to listen in and judge, but their opinion doesn't matter.

An unresolved question is a never-ending, unclarified wonder of the world. You would hate to get home and realize your homework doesn't make sense because you didn't ask. You would hate to get a quiz question on something that would have been clear if you had just asked the teacher. Who cares if the class giggles when you open your mouth? The teacher is there to help you. And it's likely others might have the same question lurking in their mind. So you not only help yourself, but possibly a fellow student by conquering your fear and asking. Stay on track and save your own giggles for the future when you're delivering your valedictorian speech to the same students that laughed at you.

When you start your career, your boss will need you to accomplish your job, and if there is a question that hinders your ability to move forward, then you need to nip the obstacle in the bud. One thing I often see in the workplace is that young professionals get nervous because they feel like they have a new question every few minutes. The last thing they want is to look like they don't know anything, but the learning curve is daunting. So instead of thinking your question is dumb, believe this: You're only dumb if you don't ask. And at least you had enough courage to conquer the fear.

Embarrassment Is a Short-Term Mindset

Sometimes the loudest cries for help are the most silent.
~ Harlan Coben

When embarrassment strikes, keep your goals in mind. You have to see the big picture and reject any negative energy in your environment that threatens to fog it up. It is important not to remain silent when you need help the most. There were countless times in school when other students made me feel less. Their remarks got the best of me sometimes. I'd feel a deep, burning pit of embarrassment that made it hard to open up. At the end of the day, I knew they didn't understand and never would.

To manage the embarrassment, I would picture myself on stage delivering the valedictorian speech. I would envision telling my story to all the people who never understood. I wanted to tell them everything I'd always wanted to but held inside. I replayed my dreams over and over in my head until one by one, they eventually started coming true. The dreams I imagined had so much more positive energy than the negativity from the embarrassment, that I became more confident in myself and what my purpose was.

By no means was this instant or easy. But the more I stayed on track and the more I kept my vision in line, the more I began to avoid feeling humiliation. It was all about staying true to myself and being disciplined. I began to see the embarrassment as short term and put it on myself to be the one to change it. I started asking myself whether any of those embarrassing moments would matter in years to come. So what if I had to ask for rides to school every day? So what if I had to ask to use other people's computers? I needed these things to help reach my goals.

I also had to learn to disregard other students' perspectives toward me. Their opinions could only hurt, not help. All the negativity was short term, but my mind was thinking years ahead.

Helpers Are There to Help

Teachers, mentors, counselors, and coaches are there to help. It's a profession they chose. Try viewing things from the perspective of the helper who wants to help you as badly as you want to be helped. Not only will the helper feel obligated, but they will feel recognized as a valuable piece to help solve your problem. Think of the helper as someone who has been waiting their entire life just to help you. It doesn't hurt to ask. There will be a mutual exchange of benefits. For example, I received just as much benefit from tutoring and drawing fun physics problems on the white board as the other students did because in helping them learn I also reinforced the material to myself.

Even though I learned this concept early in school, I still had to remind myself later in college. When I failed my chemistry lab report, I was nervous to meet with the professor. It was my first semester in a class of more than two hundred students, which was pretty daunting. I'd never met with a professor before. I didn't want to come across as dumb, and I didn't want to be one of the many students bugging her. But these were all fears I had created in my head!

I wasn't fine with failing the lab report, so I put my foot down and set up a time to discuss. The meeting ended up being an eye-opener. She said out of her two hundred students, I was the only one that made an effort to set up a meeting to discuss. She said the class average was below

70 percent. Can you believe that? The students were missing out on a great opportunity to meet directly with the person grading their assignment. I had unlocked a free help service that no one else seemed to want to try to unlock, and I ended up receiving better grades because of it.

The important lesson here is sometimes you have to step out of your comfort zone if you want to keep your goals on track. And sometimes stepping out of your comfort zone means asking around for help.

If You Never Ask, You'll Never Receive

If I never asked for rides to any of my baseball games, I believe I never would have seen baseball in my future. Through the acts of others, I was able to continue my love for the game. I ended up playing baseball until I was nineteen years old. That's eleven years of my life that I dedicate to the gracious people who got me where I needed to go. I was able to receive two scholarships to play college baseball. I even talked to the legendary Mike Martin and Mike Martin Jr. at Florida State University about the opportunity to walk-on. I made everlasting friendships and relationships with parents who opened up doors to my future. These relationships created memories that will last a lifetime. If I never asked for help, who knows where I would have ended up.

Give Thanks to Your Helpers

The best things you can ever do are be humble and give thanks to the people who take care of you. The kind nature of the human spirit makes the world go 'round. Tell your supporters how thankful you are of them, and always remember that it's okay to ask for help.

SUMMARY

- Embarrassment is a short-term mindset.
- You're only dumb if you don't ask.
- Helpers are there to help.
- If you never ask, you'll never receive.
- Give thanks to people that help.

CHAPTER 9

THE COST
OF CHEATING

Cheating is a choice, not a mistake.
~ Unknown

In college, my buddies and I referred to the students who cheated as leeches. Similar to the free-loading, parasitic nature of the leech, a cheating student lurks for its potential host to latch onto for an easy meal and free ride. In this chapter, we will examine the leech and try to answer the question: what is the cost of cheating?

Let me start by offering my definitions of the word *cheating*. Cheating is a transfer of information to a receiving body in which the received data does not get retained. It's plagiarism, the act of copying one's work and declaring it their own. It is an illusion of knowledge, a bad habit, and a key piece in the destruction of the learning development process.

Let me also make it very clear: I've cheated before. I'm not perfect. Am I proud? No. But being able to reflect on it years later, I realized the destruction and want to showcase why we should never make the choice.

Eliminate Cheating Early

Have you ever heard the saying: *Once a cheater, always a cheater?* One way or another, cheating will catch up to you, whether it's the very next day or later down the road in your career. In order to eliminate the toxic habit of cheating, it needs to be understood that there are no shortcuts to learning. With each challenge you face, there is a valuable lesson to be learned.

The next time you feel the need to peek at someone's test or copy someone's work, remind yourself that shortcuts will not maximize your true potential. If you're struggling with the classroom material or if you're rushing to meet a work deadline, this should serve as a time to reflect on your values, effort, and time management. We need to be able to answer the following questions:

Did I ask for help or try to understand the material?
What events led up to this point of needing to cheat?
What do I value more: my grade or my growth?

Sometimes it's difficult to be true to ourselves but answering simple questions in an honest manner can help foster a better sense of awareness, which plays a key role in our actions.

Skipping the beautiful inner workings of your brain's critical thinking development is adding a heftier price on your future, whether you're aware of this or not. This is very important to understand early in your life before the costs begin to add up.

Cheating Stunts Learning Development

Let's revisit one of the leeches. The leech never did his homework and didn't bother to understand the material. How did I know this?

One day, the leech approached me and asked, "Did you do homework problems four through six? Would you mind if I saw what you did?"

Being a teacher at heart, I replied, "I don't mind walking through it with you so you understand. We have a quiz on this tomorrow."

"Nah," he said. "I just need it for the homework grade."

I took a deep breath and shrugged my shoulders, as this dialogue was nothing new to me. I had dealt with these encounters for the last ten years from the same type of leeches. Each one of those homework problems took a minimum of thirty minutes to accomplish on my end, minus all of the time used to critically think about each question, reread the notes, and write out the solution. Not to mention, my professor made us submit our assignments with perfectly straight lines, neat handwriting, and underlined answers; otherwise, he would deduct points.

Regardless of the trivial nature of the homework, I was generating valuable neuron connections in the brain with each line I wrote. Every single minute of focus on the work paid dividends for the upcoming tests and for my future classes. Moving forward, each class became easier to comprehend. This is called *critical thinking development.* Think of it as a workout for your brain. When you work out your muscles they stretch and tear and ultimately grow. Your brain does the *exact* same thing.

Unfortunately for the leech, his brain avoided the gym and skipped leg day. His path may have been easier, but it was far less constructive. The leech spent five minutes copying line after line. No neurons flowed through his brain because critical thinking was never involved. His only concern was a homework grade. And as for the upcoming quiz? Yeah, he said he was going to wing it. But this was the leech's nature.

Now, one thing the leech was good at was calculating the exact grade needed to pass the class. He was smart in his own way. But how far can that system truly get you? In essence, your true values will dictate your own system. The leech's values, in this case, was the letter grade on an assignment, not learning.

As you climb the ladder of school, ask yourself what you value more: grades or growth. Let me rephrase that question to make it easier: what would you rather obtain, a letter or knowledge?

Cheating Eliminates Pride

How anxious would you feel if you were being interviewed after winning an award you cheated to get? The same can be said about the degree you'll earn after graduation. It would be difficult to look at yourself in the mirror when you know for a cold-hard fact, you did nothing on your own to achieve the honor. Also, what if you copy someone's work and they're completely wrong? Was it worth it? You failed yourself and now you have trust problems with the person you copied from. It's a double-whammy. It becomes impossible to develop pride over your work if you cheat.

We can overcome this obstacle of feeling guilty and gain more sense of pride by simply focusing on the next time around. That is all we can control. I managed by thinking about my mom watching down on me. I used her spirit as an accountability check. I never wanted to disappoint her. In high school, there were times that I did jot down other students' answers and peeked over at other students' tests. And sometimes I did share my answers with other students so they could copy. I had good intentions, but I was acting out of principle. I felt guilty. Luckily I had my mom there to serve as a check and do better the next time around.

Develop your own accountability check. This is the best way to eliminate that guilty feeling of cheating and to start having more sense of pride towards your work. Control what you can control, which is the next opportunity.

Cheating Can Get You Expelled

Once a cheater sees how easy the system may appear, it opens this new door of possibility to shortcut the system. Unfortunately, the cheater isn't jotting down the pros and cons or even thinking about the potential consequences down the road.

Something as easy as cut-and-pasting can get you expelled. Take it from me; I learned that fact the hard way during my freshman year of college. The professor assigned our class a project that would take weeks to complete based on our learning curve. The goal of the assignment was to generate an architectural set of plans for a two-story house, using a computer program we were beginners with. This was a daunting task, and the pressures of completing it—on top of the work needed in my other classes—weighed heavily. The nature of the leech bestowed its energy upon me. I wanted the easy way out, and I decided to take a short cut.

Weeks passed and the deadline approached. One of my peers at the time and I were both in the same boat: we had one day before the submittal date and had no work to show. We teamed up and split the work into two parts. I did one portion of the project, while he did the other, and then we planned to swap each other's work, turn it in, and receive our grade. At the time, it was what I needed to do to maintain my good standing in the class. After we turned in the assignment, a week passed, and I logged on to see what my grade was. As I'm scrolling through Blackboard, our college gradebook website— I get to the bottom and see in big bold:

Midterm Project = 0 percent (F)

My total grade went from an A to a C. My heart fell out of my chest. It wasn't even an hour later when I received an email from the professor. I immediately opened it with caution. It read something along the lines of:

This is a notice that you are currently under investigation for academic violation. Your standing as an engineering student will be examined over the next week by the Florida State University Board of Directors.

All of my dreams and hard work up to that point were now in the hands of a few people with no idea who I was. They didn't know the behind-the-scenes effort I put into each and every one of my classes. They only saw a small glimpse based on a costly lapse in judgment. Do you see now how something so miniscule in my head at one point ended up being major? People will only notice your one huge mistake.

For the next few weeks I was anxious about my future as an engineering student. I didn't know if I was going to be kicked out of the engineering school or expelled from FSU. The thought of letting my parents, my brother, and all the people who looked up to me clouded my mind. I could have cared less about the grade; at this point it was way more serious than a letter in a grade book. If I had just turned in my project half done, at least that would've been my own work. At least I would've had full ownership and understanding of why I received the bad grade. Except I did something far worse. So much worse that it resulted in an even greater dilemma, and I paid the hefty cost. I didn't even follow my own advice. The thought of being expelled and potentially never going back to college or starting a career was haunting.

Fortunately, my classmate and I didn't get kicked out of the engineering school after our discussion with the board of directors. A strong grade-point average and positive demeanor no doubt helped. At the end of the day, the event served as a warning and nothing more. But it was also a lesson to never break my own rules.

Cheating almost cost me my entire school career, all because I was looking for a shortcut. I embodied the nature of the leech and learned a valuable lesson along the way. I share that experience so you can avoid making the same mistake.

SUMMARY
- Eliminate the choice of cheating early.
- Cheating stunts learning development.
- Cheating makes it difficult to have pride over your work.
- The cost of cheating outweighs the reward.

CHAPTER 10

WHO CARES
ABOUT AVERAGE?

*When you're average, you're just as close to the
bottom as you are to the top.*
~ Alfred Whitehead

The words *usual, typical, ordinary, similar, standard, normal,* and
undistinguished fall under the umbrella of the term *average.* I'm not
sure about you, but I've never seen a news story flash an award of the
most *normal* person in the world. The NFL doesn't hand out a trophy for
the most *average* player of the year. Nobel Prizes don't go to the most
ordinary pieces of work.

Striving for average leaves you in the same zone as everyone else. And
if this book is in your hands, you're not trying to be like anyone else.
You're trying to harness your true potential. Working toward your true
potential separates you from your average self and ultimately makes you
unique, atypical, extraordinary, different, and special.

Engineer and visionary Elon Musk didn't have average working
hours to build his revolutionary rocket and electric vehicle companies.
NFL quarterback Tom Brady didn't develop average gameplans to win
multiple Super Bowls. Their focus is continuously aimed towards their

own individual craft and growth, and no one else's.

This chapter explores the perspective I built around the concept of average and how I built a mindset to avoid complacency, manage the stress of never feeling good enough, and end the cycle of poverty.

Who cares about average? I never have and never will.

Average Goals Yield Average Results

In sixth grade English class I heard a quote by author Norman Vincent Peale—famous for his belief in the power of positive thinking—that changed my life forever.

Shoot for the moon. Even if you miss, you'll land among the stars.

That enlightenment came at an important time because I had everything to lose. I was just a ten-year-old kid who spent the last two years in a homeless shelter looking up to the stars at night, feeling hopeless about my future. I felt just as close to the bottom as I did to the top. One slip and I would potentially continue the cycle of poverty for myself and my future family. But I had the opportunity to create my own path to never live that life again. Once I visualized education as a means to a better future, new doors opened up for me. I made the decision to press the restart button in sixth grade and created the following goals: get straight As, finish my homework before I got home, and never miss a day of school. Even with the odds against me, I was determined to aim high and land on the moon.

Even though my dad and brother fostered a strong support system, it was going to be *me* who created my own goals, showed up to class, took the tests, and learned the material. No one else could physically do that for me. Imagine if my goals were to: obtain Cs, complete 50 percent of my homework, and miss less than ten days of school. Or worse, imagine if I didn't set any goals. I might as well have been scoping out my future homeless shelters.

The worst thing we can do is not set goals for ourselves. With no goals, there are no destinations in mind. Without a destination, it's difficult to have a direction. It's like throwing darts at a dartboard with the lights off. How are we supposed to know where to aim? Adding goals to your daily operation turns the lights on. Then you can see the board, gather your darts, and begin taking aim. If I never turned the lights on in middle school, I would have continually missed the board. Maybe I'd get lucky here and there, but I couldn't afford to be inconsistent. Fortunately, I used my situation as motivation to aim high. How will you use your situation?

The second worst thing we can do is develop a love for complacency. This is the *Cs get degrees* mentality. The last thing the world needs is average engineers, doctors, politicians, scientists, musicians, etc. I find it difficult to get excited about that type of world. Where is the innovation and growth? How do we develop as a society? Will our society build average bridges? Will our doctors be average at surgery? Will our healthcare be average? What if our loved ones are crossing that bridge or are in the surgery room? Valuing a higher standard for yourself can not only help you, but it can help the world around you. We have the ability to set the standard. What type of standard would you like to set?

If you're poor or homeless, you have an edge like I did, so use it to your advantage. You have everything to lose, which should give you more purpose to not let the odds win. So set above-average goals for yourself and don't let your situation define you. Let others enjoy their security blankets, yours will arrive if you set goals and act upon them. You'll look back years later and be proud you did. Use your situation as a major plot to the story you're writing, and let your actions create a plot twist.

As for the ones with a security blanket: What else do you need?

Average Should Not Be a Checkpoint

In school a class average is a collection of data ranging from the straight-A student to the kid taking a nap in the back of the class. That data should not reflect your individual performance. Try to let your own grades be your checkpoint.

It was interesting to see students get excited about doing better than the class average because I didn't factor that metric into my measurability of progress. Instead, I compared the results of the current assignment with my previous assignments. From my perspective, this process made assignments easier to measure and control. I believe this process also helped me keep focus on myself and develop a more personal relationship with my work.

You can choose to play this endless cycle of how you're doing compared to everyone else, or you can keep track of how you're doing compared to yourself. If you get below the class average on a grade, you might feel like you're dumb, but you're not. I felt this way before, until I developed my own process. Instead of comparing yourself to the average, you should ask yourself: *What could I have done differently? What are the steps needed to avoid this next time?* Examine the test and learn from the mistakes. View your test grades as your individual check marks. It's personal, and no one else's business. It could ultimately save you heartache and mental turmoil.

I stayed on track with this mindset by not even looking at a returned test until after class. As soon as I was handed my graded test, I would immediately put it in my backpack and save it for later. I even avoided talking about grades; I absolutely hated sharing grades. There was no positive use of that information. From my perspective, I think sharing grades helped some students' egos, which didn't make sense to me because I always wanted everyone in my classes to do well, which is why I sacrificed time to tutor.

I believe competition is important for innovation and growth. However, I viewed school more as a competition with myself, rather than between me and other students. It was silly trying to be smarter than someone; what is there to prove or gain? I just wanted to learn for my own curiosity's sake. What made me feel good was measuring my own progress. Getting 1 percent better each day. My degree, the grades, and the awards were nice, but what I enjoyed the most was the battle, that was the most meaningful award. The other students weren't going to be with me during that battle waged behind closed doors and during the tests, with the countless hours and effort. That was my mentality, and I truly think it had a positive impact on my time in school.

These concepts transcend beyond the classroom. When starting your career, the only person to help your progress is you. Once I graduated college and began my career, it wasn't time to start lowering my standards. Tests, homework, and lectures disappeared, but the principle of setting a high standard was still present. Instead of studying for tests, I would stay hours late after work and learn about our software programs, engineering concepts, and anything I could find to help my career. Instead of homework, I needed to understand the process of developing a thousand-unit housing development, which took more than a forty-hour work schedule. Instead of lectures, I took precedence by setting a goal to host roundtable discussions, not only in our office, but through a live stream with the entire company. I did that because it never made sense for the business to create average products. In my case, my product is my service, so why wouldn't I aim to provide the best? What bad could that do?

My daily journal is living proof that setting above-average goals produces a desirable output. I love to review old journal entries from years ago. I may have not accomplished every single thing, but I was proud to have known I did everything I could. There is always something to be learned along the way. How will you begin to measure your own goals?

I never wanted to be typical. Typical was boring, posed no challenge, and I simply couldn't afford it. I often asked myself: *What more can I do? How crazy would it be if I did that?* But it was only crazy until it came to fruition.

SUMMARY
- Average goals yield average results.
- Do not let average be a checkpoint.
- Avoid complacency and aim high.

CHAPTER 11

LEAVE A
POSITIVE TIMELINE

Such is the power, the stupendous power, of sincere,
heartfelt appreciation.
~ Dale Carnegie, How to Win Friends and Influence People

To those who truly know who I am, they know that I'm silly, playful, and a little brother at heart. If I can make someone laugh, make them feel important, or teach someone something new, then I know I have done something positive. That's the type of timeline I strive to leave behind.

And I'm not perfect. I've made people upset. I've said the wrong things. But I also have a second chance to make a conscious effort of how I leave my timeline behind the next time around.

Which timeline would be the most beneficial to leave behind: positive or negative?

You won't be able to please everyone, and some people don't plan on pleasing everyone. But this isn't about pleasing others. This is about you. If you want to create the most benefit and opportunity for yourself, perhaps the best side to pick is to leave something positive behind.

Leaving a Positive Timeline Doesn't Do Any Bad, Only Good

I'm sure we've all walked away from a conversation or encounter and thought: *Wow, that person was rude.* Maybe someone didn't say thank you, maybe they made a snarky remark, maybe their word choice was insensitive, or whatever the case. Regardless, you felt a certain way.

What good does that type of timeline bring to the world?

Doing the exact opposite can only do good.

Treat others the way you want to be treated

Every single day of elementary school, my principal would conclude his morning announcement with: *And remember students, treat others the way you want to be treated.* It became so consistent that all of the students would harmonize with him.

Imagine if every single kid in the country continued that philosophy for the rest of their lives; the world would be such an amazing place. If you're reading this, remember it's never too late to join the pact. The best thing you can ever do for your name is to leave moments of positivity and respect when hanging out with people. Just smiling and saying: *Thank you, I really appreciate it* can go a long way.

If I had left a negative timeline when growing up, I wouldn't be here to share my story. But that was dependent on me keeping that consistency through little things like saying thank you, telling people I appreciated them, and making a conscious effort to be kind. I believed people were more willing to help me because of my own efforts.

Next time you're in class, at work, or at the store, try harnessing the power of sincere gratitude and see what happens. You might be surprised with the good it brings.

People remember you by the way you make them feel

My brother once told me that early on, and it stuck with me ever since. People's perceptions of you are built from the accumulation of interactions you've exchanged with them over time. They may not remember exactly every word you've said but they will remember how you made them feel. In that case, wouldn't it be beneficial to make people feel good?

Your word choice, your mannerisms, and your energy are on centerstage. How you move through time is being recorded in their eyes. You leave a little part of your timeline with each and every moment.

I've never heard a bad thing said about an open-minded, respectful, down-to-earth person. And by open-minded, I mean you're engaging, you're asking questions, you're sympathizing, you're trying to see the other perspective. You're putting each topic on trial and viewing all angles, rather than believing there's only one side to it. You're throwing away all preconceived notions for the time being. Nothing is right or wrong; it just is. There are fewer arguments, but more evaluations. Nothing is black or white, red, or blue. If you're looking from the outside of the box, there are no sides. Henry Ford said it best: "If there is any one secret of success, it lies in the ability to get to another person's point of view and see things from that person's angles as well as from your own."

The Earth wasn't built only for you. There are other people, perspectives, hardships, and stories. Listen to them and you might learn something new, because they'll remember how you made them feel.

You Can't Please Everyone

Being kind is a choice. And let's face it, some people are allergic to kindness. All people have their own problems, concerns, pain, and perspectives of life. Unfortunately, they will be stuck in their ways for eternity, wreaking negative energy until they *choose* to make a change.

Living life trying to please others isn't the route people want to go. But we can't view this as pleasing others. This isn't about them; it's about you. This is your timeline. If leaving a negative timeline is something you want to do, no one is stopping you. You have the choice to disrespect others or simply not care about anyone.

However, a negative timeline may not foster the future you're searching for. If you have goals of graduating at the top of your class, going to college, starting your own business, being a professional athlete, people will always remember the way you made them feel. And depending on whether that was a positive or a negative experience could make or break the foundation of that relationship you're trying to build.

You have the option of representing the person you want to be. What type of timeline would you like to leave?

SUMMARY
- Leaving a positive timeline only does good, not bad.
- People remember how you make them feel, so make them feel good.
- You can't please everyone but it isn't about them; it's about you.

FINAL MESSAGE

Nearly every kid has had that moment when they said: *When I grow up, I want to be* (fill in the blank).

But some lose that dream. They lose their vision. The mindset gets crowded. The confidence gets destroyed. The influences around them grab control. And to the ones who are poor or homeless, their cycle continues; the statistics don't lie. For those not in poverty, some lose their true potential and take life's opportunities for granted.

I know what it feels like to be isolated, embarrassed, and defeated. I also know what it feels like to be on top of the world and collapse right on my face. But I never quit telling myself: *When I grow up I want to be...* This was a choice. Even with the odds against me, the power of mindset defied every statistic. When I was growing up, I wanted my voice heard, and now I have the privilege of sharing my story with you.

No matter the odds, no matter how defeated you feel, and no matter what obstacle you face next, never lose sight of the dream you had as a kid. And most importantly: *never give up.*

APPENDIX FACTS AND STATS ABOUT HOMELESS STUDENTS

According to the McKinney-Vento Homeless Assistance Act: homeless students are defined as students who lack a fixed, regular, and adequate nighttime residence, that is, students living in shared housing, hotels or motels, shelters, and unsheltered places such as cars, parks, abandoned buildings.

How many homeless students are there in the United States?

Since 2008, the number of homeless students identified by public schools each year has increased by more than 100 percent, from approximately 680,000 to 1,384,000 students in 2019.[1]

Where do homeless students sleep?

In the 2018-19 school year, approximately 77 percent of homeless students lived in doubled-up or shared housing due to loss of housing, economic hardship, or other reasons such as domestic violence; 12 percent lived in shelters, transitional housing, or awaiting foster care; 7 percent lived in hotels or motels, and 4 percent were unsheltered living in cars, parks, campgrounds, temporary trailers—including Federal Emergency Management Agency (FEMA) trailers—or abandoned buildings.[2]

How do homeless students perform in the classroom?

Some research shows that only 64 percent of homeless students

---

[1] https://www.nsba.org/Perspectives/2021/homeless-students
[2] Ibid

graduate from high school, compared to a national average of 78 percent for low-income students and 84 percent for all students. According to one report, students experiencing homelessness are 87 percent more likely to drop out of school than their stably housed peers. Other research states that without a high school diploma, youth are 4.5 times more likely to experience homelessness later in life.[3]

Homeless students are less likely to take AP exams

Students who experienced homelessness in high school were more likely to attend a school that offered no AP courses compared to students who were always housed (19 percent vs. 12 percent). At the same time, homeless students were far less likely to attend a school that offered a variety of AP courses (six or more) than housed students (34 percent vs. 53 percent).

Across all subject areas, homeless students who took AP exams were less likely to pass them than their housed classmates, though the discrepancy varied by subject.[4]

Reasons why homeless students aren't college ready: chronic absenteeism, midyear transfers, mental health.

This includes addressing the reasons homeless students often fall behind in their learning, which can be traced back to a student's early school years: the compounding effects of chronic absenteeism, midyear transfers, late identification of additional education needs, and mental and physical health issues such as depression or asthma on academic performance. Homeless students, especially those who experience frequent chronic absenteeism and school transfers, often do not have an opportunity to catch up to classmates and perform at grade level even

---

[3] Ibid
[4] Ibid

after they return to permanent housing. This makes them less likely to graduate or be prepared for college-level coursework.[5]

---

[5] https://www.icphusa.org/reports/beyond-graduation/#how-do-homeless-students-perform-in-advanced-placement-classes-

BIBLIOGRAPHY

Cai, Jinghong. "Homeless Students in Public Schools across America: Down but Not Out." National School Board Association, July 27, 2021. https://www.nsba.org/Perspectives/2021/homeless-students.

Carnegie, Dale. *How to Win Friends and Influence People*. New York: Simon and Shuster, 1981.

Dweck, Carol S. *Mindset*. New York: Ballantine Books, 2016.

Kennedy, Terri. "The Power of Perspective." *Huffington Post*, October 10, 2011. https://www.huffpost.com/entry/positive-attitude-advice_b_1018175.

Kiewra, Kenneth A. "Providing the instructor's notes: An effective addition to student note taking." *Educational Psychologist* 20, no. 1 (1985): 33–39. doi.org/10.1207/s15326985ep2001_5

Maxwell, John C. *The 15 Invaluable Laws of Growth*. New York: Hachette Book Group, 2012.

Nye, Pauline A., Terence J. Crooks, Melanie Powley, and Gail Tripp. "Student note-taking related to university examination performance." *Higher Education* 13, no. 1 (1984): 85–97. doi.org/10.1007/BF00136532.

Rennie, Jon S. *All In The Same Boat*. Wake Forest, NC: Deck and Conn, 2021.

www.ingramcontent.com/pod-product-compliance
Lightning Source LLC
Chambersburg PA
CBHW020421130626
46549CB00006B/2677